# Spotlight on
# Neutrals

## Quilts and More for Any Decor

### Pat Wys

*Martingale*®
& COMPANY

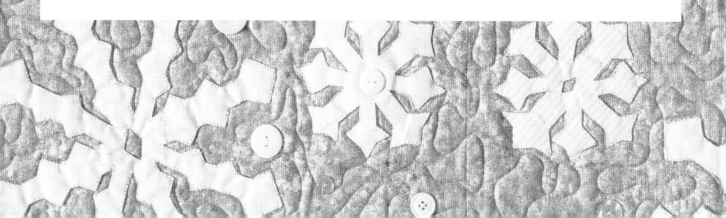

Spotlight on Neutrals:
Quilts and More for Any Decor
© 2011 by Pat Wys

That Patchwork Place® is an imprint
of Martingale & Company®.

Martingale & Company
19021 120th Ave. NE, Suite 102
Bothell, WA 98011
www.martingale-pub.com

Printed in China
16 15 14 13 12          8 7 6 5 4 3 2

**Library of Congress Cataloging-in-Publication
Data is available upon request.**

ISBN: 978-1-60468-050-8

## Credits

President & CEO: Tom Wierzbicki

Editorial Director: Mary V. Green

Managing Editor: Karen Costello Soltys

Technical Editor: Nancy Mahoney

Copy Editor: Melissa Bryan

Design Director: Stan Green

Production Manager: Regina Girard

Illustrator: Adrienne Smitke

Cover & Text Designer: Regina Girard

Photographer: Brent Kane

## Mission Statement

*Dedicated to providing quality products
and service to inspire creativity.*

*To love and be loved is to feel the sun from both sides.*

David Viscott, MD

There is no way I could adequately express the love I have for my husband, daughters, and new son-in-law. This book is dedicated to my family, with a message to each.

First and most important, to Andy, the love of my life. We have spent a lifetime raising our family and enjoying all that this world has to give. You are the reason for everything good in my life. You are my best friend and the safety net below me at all times. Your complete and unselfish dedication to our family is an example of what a man, husband, and father should be. You have encouraged and supported me and stepped out of the way to let me fly. Thank you, my love.

To Emily, whose beauty and incredible joy for life are amazing. You light up a room when you walk through the door. I am a proud mother. Thank you for loving and supporting me and all my creative endeavors. You are one fabulous young woman. We are best friends now!

To Mary Beth, so beautiful and unique! You are strong, you set goals and achieve those goals, and I'm so proud of you. I love your gentle spirit and depth of understanding about everything. Where does that calm wisdom come from at such a young age? Thank you for loving me and encouraging me in everything I do. You are one fabulous young woman. We are best friends now!

To Russ, the new son in my life! You are part of our family and part of our hearts. I love the way you love my daughter (and my quilts). God has blessed us with you. We will always be there for you. We are family.

18

35

22

40

28

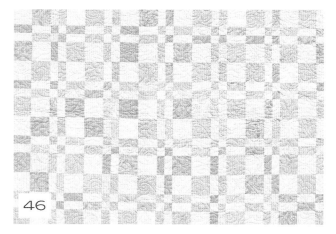

46

33

51

55

60

64

Contents

*Why not go out on a limb?*
*Isn't that where the fruit is?*

Frank Sculty

I love quilting, quilts, and most of all quilters. Big shock! I love every single color, including all the shades, tints, and hues within the color spectrum. I love prints large and small, from vintage to whimsical. My taste in color and fabric changes regularly. Many thanks to the fabulous fabric industry for keeping it coming! I guess you can say I'm all over the board; I don't specialize in any one area or genre, and I don't have too much trouble stepping outside the box. A few years ago I realized that when I visit quilt shops, I peruse the neutral fabrics first. I began thinking of making an all-neutral quilt, and "White Chocolate" (page 18) was my first endeavor. This book represents the compilation and celebration of my love of neutral fabrics.

When I began this book-writing journey, I set two goals for myself. The first was to throw open the doors of possibility and get quilters to rethink the use and purpose of neutral fabrics. Let's think of neutrals as the stars of the show, instead of the supporting cast. The second was to create a book that would be an enjoyable reading experience. My thoughts and feelings will be evident throughout the pages, and I hope you will find plenty to keep you both entertained and informed.

So, what defines a neutral? Very simply, a neutral is anything that does not appear on the color wheel. From black to white, from brown to cream, and encompassing all the shades and tints in between—those are neutrals. There are more choices than you think! I went to the quilt show in Paducah vowing to purchase only neutral fabrics. I came home with 122 different neutral fabrics and a huge dent in my credit card. I even decided to purchase neutral silk fabric, which I used in the quilt "French Silk" (page 28) and in the mantel scarf "Winter Solstice Mantel Scarf" (page 64). I loved the look and will definitely use silk again in future quilts. When you begin looking at neutrals with a different eye, you won't believe what is out there in the fabric world.

The decorating scheme in each bedroom of my home began with a neutral quilt. A quilt sets the stage for the decor and provides plenty of options for changing the look of the room with paint color and seasonal accents. I use neutral quilts as both the focus and the stage for my ever-growing collection of quilts. With neutral elements on beds and pieces of furniture I can change out colorful quilts, pillows, table runners, and wall hangings as much as I like. The versatility of neutrals is amazing.

Neutrals are timeless, always available, and not necessarily "line specific." They stand alone in their own very special genre. I'm drawn to neutrals by their design depth—the simplicity of some and complexity of others. Fabric manufacturers have given us some gorgeous neutral fabrics with which to work. Most recently, I have seen an even bigger presence of neutrals in new fabrics; additionally, whole collections of neutrals continue to be developed and are very popular. I believe that neutrals are coming into their own and will stand alone with beautiful quilts and projects. It's my sincere hope that you'll take a closer look at neutrals and the possibilities of using these super fabrics in your quilt collection.

This primer is designed to be used as a reference tool as you make the quilts in this book and other projects along the way. Even if you have a PhD in quilting, it's good to revisit the standard techniques. You never know when you might find something new! If you're a beginner, this section will help reinforce the techniques you're just learning until they become a comfortable part of your quilting routines. Welcome to the classroom.

### The Value of Value

When choosing fabrics with a neutral palette, close attention needs to be paid to value. Value is the relative degree of lightness or darkness in a color. From the palest to the darkest, and every shade in between, value comes into play to give your projects depth and sparkle.

In this book, I refer to the fabrics in terms of value. For example, in the cutting list for each project you'll be instructed to cut "From the light-value fabrics" or "From the medium- and dark-value fabrics." This is where the rubber meets the road in any quilt, but it is particularly important when using neutrals. When you combine fabrics with the same or nearly the same value, you get a blended quilt. When you mix light and dark values, you create contrast. Some of the quilts in this book are low in contrast while others are higher. Think about the final quilt and the look you want to achieve. Do you want high contrast with tons of sparkle? Then choose very dark fabrics and put them right next to very light fabrics. Do you want a subtle partnership of fabric as if you were stirring a mixing bowl of paint, gradually blending two or three shades? Then choose fabrics with nearly the same color value and put them together. It's all about the depth of color saturation.

### Plan Ahead

Here is a groundbreaking piece of advice. Before you start any project, do this first: Brew yourself a cup of tea, sit down, and *read the pattern!* You probably think I'm being dramatic, but I'm not kidding. Read, make notes, and plan ahead. I believe that if quilters would read a pattern thoroughly and carefully, a huge percentage of mistakes in the quilting process could be avoided.

Plan the fabrics you want to use and where you want to use them. Make snippet charts and notes along the way. When you cut the pieces for a unit, pin together the fabrics that will be sewn together. That way you won't go wrong. Plastic zip-top bags are readily available in the grocery store and are a handy tool for keeping pieces organized.

If you have to interrupt your project before it's finished (life does that to us), mark the place in the book where you stopped, and then pin a note to the corresponding point in your sewn pieces. You can pick up easily where you left off, if you take this one little step.

It's always a good idea to make a sample block from your scraps. Sample blocks help make you aware of any pitfalls you might encounter later on. And there's no need to waste the sample block. You can use it as a label for the back of the quilt.

The time you spend on planning your quilt will come back to you in the construction process. An organized project is a project less likely to have problems. Ask me how I know!

## Prewashing Fabrics

I hope the quilt police are busy elsewhere when I make this confession: I don't always prewash my fabrics (although I know I probably should). Dye-catcher sheets available in grocery stores, special quilt-fabric detergents found in quilt shops, and a dye-setting product called Retayne have all made it easy to skip prewashing. You can use these products to wash a quilt *after* it's finished without worrying about bleeding, even if you didn't prewash the fabrics. I use them all and have not had any problems with fabric bleeding. Besides, I love the wrinkly, vintage-looking way my quilts turn out when they're washed after being quilted.

## Pressing

I'm a major presser. I seem to spend as much time with an iron in my hand as I spend sewing. I use steam and press the fabric pieces before I begin cutting. This is important because if the fabric is going to shrink or expand, I want it to happen before I start cutting. After sewing a seam, I first press the stitched line on the wrong side. Then I flip the pieces open and press the seam allowances from the right side, in whichever direction my pattern indicates.

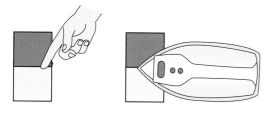

Most of the time I press seam allowances to one side, but occasionally I'll press them open to reduce bulk. The one time I always press the seam allowances open is when I join strips with a diagonal seam, particularly for binding. I want that seam to be as flat as I can get it.

### PRESSING FOR SUCCESS

When two units are being stacked and sewn together, it's always preferable to have opposing seams. This is where it becomes important to pay close attention to the direction in which seam allowances are pressed. If the seams don't line up perfectly you may need to do some "easin' and squeezin'," adjusting the top and bottom layers so that they nestle together. Extra pinning helps too!

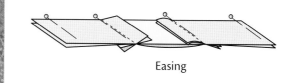

Easing

## Cutting

Never underestimate the power of a sharp rotary cutter. I use the two-ruler method for making the first cut in my fabric. Note that the following rotary-cutting instructions are written for right-handers; reverse the instructions if you're left-handed.

1. Press the fabric and then fold it in half, matching the selvages. Place the fabric on your cutting mat with the folded edge closest to your body. Align a square ruler with the fold of the fabric and place a long ruler to the left so that the raw edges of the fabric are covered. Remove the square ruler and make a rotary cut along the right edge of the long ruler. Then, without disturbing the fabrics, remove the long ruler and discard the waste strip. This is known as a cleanup cut.

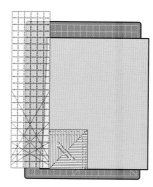 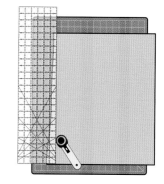

2. To cut strips, align the desired strip width on the ruler with the newly cut edge of the fabric. Rolling the cutter away from you, cut along the right edge of the ruler, from the fold to the selvage. Walk the

fingers of your left hand along the ruler as you cut to help prevent the ruler from slipping.

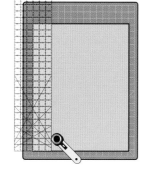

> ### CHECK AND STRAIGHTEN
>
> When cutting a lot of strips from one fabric, at some point you'll need to make a new cleanup cut. Some people think you should make a fresh cut after three or four strips; I don't make one that often, however. I make a cleanup cut when I detect the fabric is "off" a bit, or when the cut edge is not an exact right angle to the folded edge of the fabric. I let the fabric tell me when it's time to straighten the cut edge.

3. To cut squares and rectangles, first cut a strip of the desired width, removing the selvage ends. Align the required measurement on the ruler with the left edge of the strip and cut a square or rectangle, as desired. Continue cutting until you have the required number of pieces.

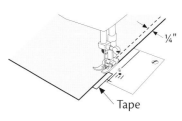

## Piecing (aka Drive Carefully!)

For quilting projects, use a ¼" seam allowance. It's a good idea to mark a ¼"-wide seam guide on your sewing machine. You can create a guide using painter's tape or one of the many other aids available. Remember to check the accuracy of your seam guide

regularly, particularly after you have cleaned your machine or changed the needle.

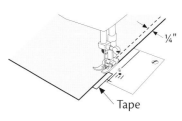

## Seam Test

Here is a handy little test for checking ¼" seam accuracy.

1. Cut three strips of fabric, 1½" x 3".

2. Sew the strips together using what you believe to be your most accurate guide for sewing a ¼"-wide seam allowance.

3. Press the seam allowances toward outside strips.

4. Measure the center strip; it should measure exactly 1" wide. The three-strip unit should measure 3½" x 3". If it doesn't, adjust the seam guide in the proper direction and repeat the test.

## Pin, Pin, Pin

I'm a pinner. I pin like crazy, but I must offer a word of caution: There are pins, and then there are harpoons. Don't use pins that could take down Shamu the whale! They take up too much volume in the fabric and will affect the accuracy of your piecing. Thin pins make a huge difference in holding your units together and helping you sew effectively. I love silk pins . . . a lot!

## Chain, Chain, Chain

Learning to chain piece is the biggest time-saver in quiltmaking. Now that you have done the advance planning with your fabrics, stack and chain piece whenever possible. Simply feed the pieces through the machine without clipping the threads between the pieces. When finished, clip and press the pieces following the pressing guidelines. Use scraps of fabric or quilt units at the beginning and end of a chain.

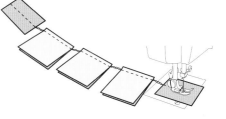

End sewing with
a thread saver.

## Making Half-Square-Triangle Units

I make these units using two squares, instead of cutting triangles. I also cut the squares slightly oversized, which makes them easier to cut and sew. You can trim and square up the resulting units to the correct size afterward.

1. Cut the squares 1" larger than the desired finished size of the half-square-triangle unit. For example, if you want a 3" finished half-square-triangle unit, start with two squares, 4" x 4". The size to cut is indicated in the cutting directions for individual projects.

2. Layer the squares right sides together in pairs, with the lighter color on top. Draw a diagonal line on the wrong side of the lighter square. Stitch ¼" from both sides of the drawn line.

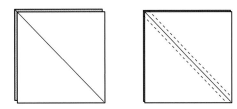

3. Cut the squares apart on the drawn line. Press the seam allowances toward the darker triangle, unless instructed otherwise. You will have two half-square-triangle units.

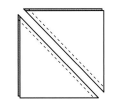

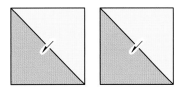

4. Using one of the units and a square ruler with a 45° line, place the 45° line on top of the seam line, making sure the raw edges on all sides of the unit extend beyond the required measurements on the ruler. Trim two sides as shown. Rotate the unit, aligning the required measurement on the ruler with the just-trimmed edges and the 45° line with the seam line. Trim the other two sides. (I know

this is an extra step, but your half-square-triangle units will be perfectly sized and the edges will be neat and clean.)

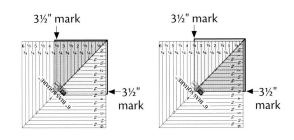

3½" mark     3½" mark

◄ 3½" mark     ◄ 3½" mark

---

### ACHIEVING PERFECTION

I believe the single most important action you can take to ensure the perfection of your units, blocks, and quilts is to square up the pieces throughout the quiltmaking process. This step alone might not *guarantee* a pristine result, but I can guarantee you won't achieve perfection without it!

---

## Making Quarter-Square-Triangle Units

As with half-square-triangle units, I prefer to make quarter-square-triangle units without cutting triangles.

1. Cut two squares 1½" larger than the desired finished unit.

2. Follow steps 2 and 3 of "Making Half-Square-Triangle Units" at left. Make two half-square-triangle units, but don't trim them to size yet.

3. On the wrong side of one of the units, draw a line diagonally from corner to corner as shown.

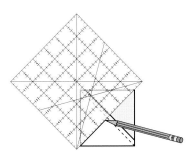

4. Place the half-square-triangle units right sides together. Make sure contrasting fabrics are facing each other and the marked square is on top. Butt the diagonal seams against each other and pin to secure. Sew ¼" from both sides of the drawn line,

and then cut the units apart on the line to make two quarter-square-triangle units.

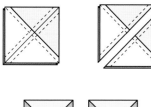

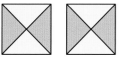

5. Square up the units as described in step 4 of "Making Half-Square-Triangle Units," making sure both sides of the ruler line up where the two fabrics intersect as shown.

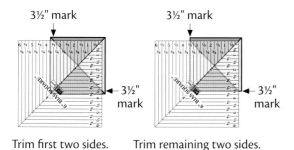

3½" mark                3½" mark

←3½"                    ←3½"
mark                    mark

Trim first two sides.    Trim remaining two sides.

## Squaring Up Blocks

Just as you square up the units, take the time to square up your completed blocks. Sometimes this process is nothing more than a checkpoint to see if each block is the right size, and sometimes you are merely giving the blocks a little haircut! Either way, this precaution is a very good thing.

Measure the blocks and make sure they are the desired size plus an exact ¼" on each edge for seam allowances. Trim larger blocks to match the size of smaller ones. If your blocks are not the required finished size, adjust all the other components of the quilt accordingly.

Follow these steps to trim the blocks:

1. Place a large square ruler on top of the block, making sure the raw edges on all sides of the block extend beyond the desired measurements on the ruler and that there is a ¼" beyond the outermost points for seam allowance. Trim away the excess that extends beyond the ruler on the right edge and top edge of the block.

2. Rotate the block 180° and align the desired measurement on the ruler with the just-trimmed edges of the block. Trim the remaining two sides.

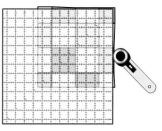

## Dispersing Seams Evenly

When you have four seams intersecting in the center of a unit or block, it's a good idea to reduce the bulk by creating opposing seams where the seams come together. After the seam is sewn, use a seam ripper to remove two or three stitches from the seam allowance on *both* sides of the center seam as shown. Reposition both seam allowances to evenly distribute the fabric, and press the seam allowances in opposite directions so that the center lies flat. When you look at the wrong side of the block, the seam allowances should be going in one direction, either clockwise or counterclockwise around the center.

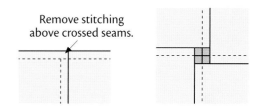

Remove stitching above crossed seams.

## Folded Corners

The folded-corner technique is a common way to achieve a triangle-shaped corner by layering one square on top of a larger square. Use the following steps to make folded-corner units for Snowball and Square in a Square blocks.

1. Draw a diagonal line from corner to corner on the wrong side of the smaller square.

2. Place the marked square on one corner of a larger square, right sides together. Pin the marked square in place if needed.

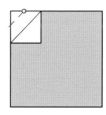

3. Stitch along the drawn line, a width of just one or two threads from the line, on what will be the seam-allowance side of the line. Doing this compensates for the slight inaccuracy caused when pressing the unit.

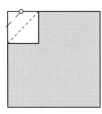

4. Before trimming, press the resulting triangle open so that it lines up perfectly with the edges of the underlying square. If the edges don't match, sew the line again! Fold back the top triangle and trim away both of the remaining excess triangles, leaving a ¼" seam allowance.

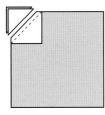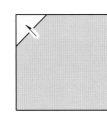

### MAKE USE OF THE WASTE

You can make bonus half-square-triangle units by sewing another line of stitching ½" from the first stitched line. Cut between the two stitched lines and press the seam allowances toward the darker fabric.

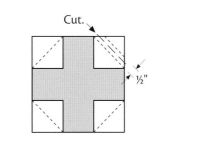

Cut.

½"

## Appliqué

I adore appliqué in any form. In my perfect world I would hand appliqué everything using traditional needle-turn methods. However, other methods do have their advantages. For "Kitty's Baskets" (page 71), I used machine appliqué and prepared the motifs with freezer paper. For the snowflakes shapes in "Baby It's Cold Outside" (page 60) and "Winter Solstice Mantel Scarf" (page 64), I used raw-edge appliqué. Both methods are described in this section. I saved time by sewing the shapes using a very small machine blanket stitch. In "Baby It's Cold Outside," I used monofilament for the first time and loved it.

### Supplies for Machine Appliqué

.004 monofilament (polyester *not* nylon), clear and smoke

Fabric glue stick

Small scissors

Freezer paper

Small iron (easier to use than a full-sized iron)

Open-toe presser foot

Size 75/11 machine needles

### Preparing for Freezer-Paper Appliqué

1. Trace the specified number of appliqué shapes onto the dull side of freezer paper. Carefully cut out the shapes, cutting directly on the drawn lines. For extra stability, you can make a second freezer-paper template of each shape. Then, with the shiny side of one freezer-paper template next to the dull side of the other template, lightly press a spot in the middle of the two templates. The templates will easily stick together for a double-thick template.

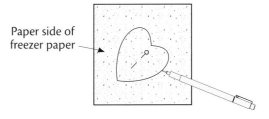

Paper side of freezer paper

2. Use a fabric glue stick to apply a small amount of glue to the dull side of each freezer-paper template. Affix the template to the wrong side of the

fabric, leaving about ½" between shapes for seam allowances.

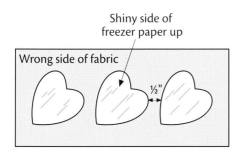

Shiny side of
freezer paper up

Wrong side of fabric

½"

3. Cut out each shape using small, sharp scissors, adding a scant ¼" seam allowance around the edges.

4. Using a small iron, press the seam allowances onto the shiny part of the freezer paper. The plastic coating will act as a temporary fixative and hold the seam allowances in place. Clip the seam allowances on all curves, stopping one or two threads from the edge of the freezer-paper template.

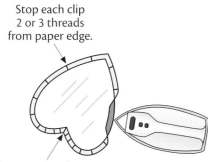

Stop each clip
2 or 3 threads
from paper edge.

Clip to paper edge.

5. For outer points, press the seam allowance so that the folded edge of the fabric extends beyond the point of the freezer paper.

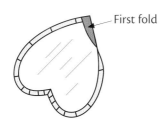

First fold

6. Apply a small amount of fabric glue to the inside fold of the fabric at the point. Then fold over the seam allowance and continue pressing.

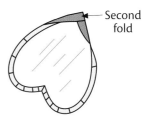

Second
fold

7. For inner points, clip at the innermost point and use the iron to fuse the two sides of the point to the freezer-paper template.

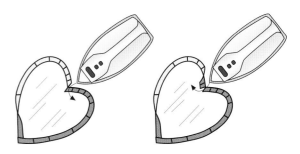

8. When you've finished, check the prepared appliqué to make sure the edges are smooth and flat. If needed, go back and fix any areas that need some re-pressing.

### Preparing for Raw-Edge Appliqué

I chose raw-edge appliqué (also known as fusible appliqué) for both "Baby It's Cold Outside" (page 60) and "Winter Solstice Mantel Scarf" (page 64) because I wanted a fast, fun method for those projects. With raw-edge appliqué, you normally draw or trace your templates in reverse. The snowflake patterns are symmetrical, however, and don't need to be reversed. If you want to use this method for "Kitty's Baskets" (page 71), you will need to reverse the asymmetrical shapes. Simply trace the shapes onto a piece of paper, place the paper against a bright window with the traced side toward the light, and trace the shape onto the back of the paper.

Refer to the manufacturer's instructions when applying fusible web to your fabrics. Follow these additional steps, and you'll have your project at the finish line very soon.

1. Trace or draw the shape onto the paper-backing side of the fusible web.

2. Roughly cut out the shape, leaving about a ¼" margin all around the outline. For larger shapes, cut out the center of the fusible-web shape, leaving a scant ¼" inside the line. This trimming allows the shape to adhere to the background while eliminating stiffness within the shape.

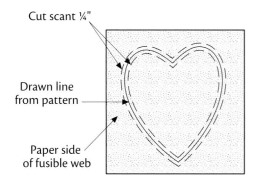

Cut scant ¼"

Drawn line from pattern

Paper side of fusible web

3. Place the shape, fusible-web side down, on the wrong side of the fabric. Fuse in place.

4. Cut out the shape exactly on the marked line.

5. Remove the paper backing, place the shape on the right side of the background fabric, and press in place.

6. When all the shapes are fused, finish the raw edges with a decorative stitch, such as a machine blanket stitch as described in the following section.

### Stitching the Appliqué

You can use this stitching technique with either freezer-paper or raw-edge appliqué. I recommend making a test piece with fabric scraps to check your stitches. Sew one or two rows of blanket or zigzag stitches, and adjust your stitch length and width as needed to achieve the desired results.

1. Start by sewing small straight stitches in the background, very close to the appliqué shape, for approximately 1". Then change to a blanket (or zigzag) stitch and continue sewing around the shape.

2. Use the needle-down feature on your machine, or the hand wheel, so that the needle always stops in the down position when stopping or pivoting for curves, outer corners, and inner points. Continue stitching around the shape until you reach the point where you started the blanket (or zigzag) stitches. End with a few very small straight stitches to anchor your threads. This creates a smooth and nearly invisible transition from beginning to end.

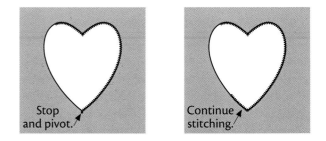

Stop and pivot.

Continue stitching.

3. If you used the freezer-paper method, you'll need to remove the paper when the appliqué is complete. Use small scissors to carefully cut away the background fabric behind the appliqué shape, leaving approximately ¼" for seam allowance. The paper template should release easily.

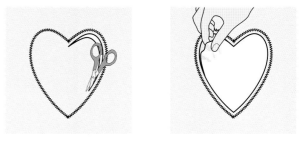

## Finishing School

The quilt is almost complete. Now it's time to consider all that goes into bringing your project to the finishing line. Accurate sewing and measuring are just as important during these final stages as when you were sewing the basic units during block construction.

### Adding Borders

Borders add the final exclamation point to any quilt project. Whether they are intricately pieced, or just plain strips of complementary fabric, borders make a statement. Follow these guidelines for sewing borders to your projects.

In general, I prefer to add border strips to the longer sides first, and then attach them to the remaining two sides.

1. Measure the length of the quilt top through the center and also 3" or 4" from both outer edges. If the measurements differ, calculate the average by adding the three measurements together and then dividing by three.

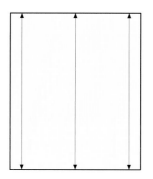

Measure in three places.

## JOINING STRIPS

If you cut strips from the crosswise grain and you don't have a strip of fabric long enough for a border or binding, you'll need to join the strips with a diagonal seam to make a long, continuous strip. To do this, join strips at right angles, right sides together, and stitch diagonally across the corner as shown. Trim the excess fabric, leaving a ¼" seam allowance, and press the seam allowances open. You'll get a very flat strip, which is particularly nice when joining strips for binding.

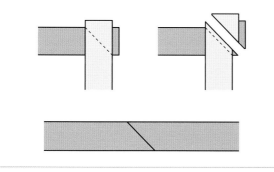

2. Cut two border strips to the length determined in step 1, piecing as necessary. Mark or pin the center of the border strips and the center of the sides of the quilt top. With right sides together, pin the border strips to the sides of the quilt, matching centers and ends. (Depending on the size of the quilt, you may want to fold the quilt top and border

strips into quarters, mark the quarter-points, and then add more pins, matching the quarter-points.) Using a ¼"-wide seam allowance, sew the side borders to the quilt, easing as needed. Press the seam allowances toward the border strips.

3. Repeat the process for the top and bottom borders, measuring across the side borders you just added when determining the quilt width.

### Basting and Quilting

The choices in finishing your quilt are limitless. There is hand quilting—timeless, lovely, and oh-so-cuddly. Within the world of hand quilting there is big-stitch quilting, which I used in "Kitty's Baskets" (page 71). Then we have the amazing realm of long-arm quilting. I love the beauty and intricacy of projects completed by long-arm experts. They make my work look so good, my heart stops! And, of course, there is the option of machine quilting on the sewing machine. It's so much fun to practice new skills and use all the capabilities our modern machines have to offer. Whether you choose to quilt by hand or by sewing machine, here are a few steps of preparation to make the process easy.

1. Place the backing fabric wrong side up on a flat surface. Use tape or clamps to anchor the backing so that it's taut but not stretched out of shape.

2. Place the batting over the backing, smoothing out any wrinkles.

3. Center the pressed quilt top on top of the batting and backing. Smooth out any wrinkles and make sure the quilt-top edges are parallel to the edges of the backing.

4. Starting in the center and working toward the outer edges, pin through all the layers with rust-proof safety pins. Place the pins 4" to 5" apart, avoiding areas where you intend to quilt.

5. When basting is complete, remove the tape or clamps and quilt away.

### Binding

I'm going to say it, I'm going to put it down in words right here. I prefer bias binding in almost every situation. Why? For several reasons. First, for the longevity of the quilt; I believe it's more durable. Second, for subtleness along the edges; the quilt is softer and drapes so nicely. And third, for ease of application and construction.

In my workshops and lectures people tell me that bias binding is difficult to make and takes too long. Use these steps and you'll find it doesn't take one minute longer to cut bias binding than straight-edge binding. Plus, is there anything prettier than a stripe or plaid on the bias around the edges of a quilt?

1. Place the fabric rectangle or square flat on your rotary-cutting mat with the wrong side facing up. Note the numbered corners in the diagram below.

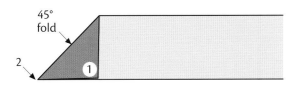

2. Fold corner 1 down to the bottom edge, creating a bias fold line at a 45° angle across the fabric.

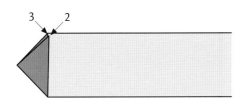

3. Bring corner 2 up to point 3, folding the bias edge onto itself.

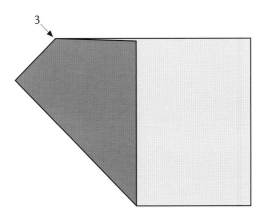

4. If you're using a full width of fabric, you'll need to make another fold by bringing the bias point up to point 3. (If you have less than a full width of fabric, you might not need to make this additional fold.)

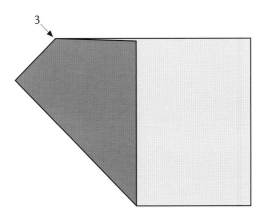

5. Rotate the fabric so that the last folded edge is closest to you. Trim off the fold and then cut strips of the desired width. The projects in this book call for strips that are 2½" wide, but you can use any width you prefer. Cut enough strips to go around the quilt top, plus about 12".

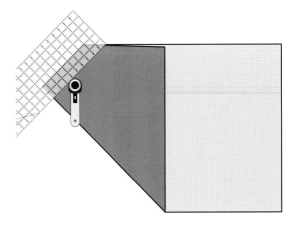

6. With right sides together, sew the strips into one long strip, offsetting the seams by ¼" as shown. Press the seam allowances open. Fold the strip in half lengthwise, wrong sides together, and press.

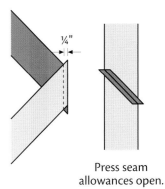

Press seam allowances open.

7. Starting on one side of the quilt (not in a corner), align the raw edge of the strip with the raw edge of the quilt top. Using a walking foot and a ¼"-wide seam allowance, stitch the binding to the quilt, leaving a 6" tail unstitched where you start. Stop stitching ¼" from the corner, and with the needle in the down position, pivot at a 45° angle and stitch to the outer corner of the quilt.

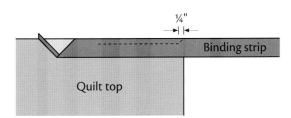

8. Clip the threads and remove the quilt from the sewing machine. Fold the binding straight up, away from the quilt, making a 45° angle. Fold the binding back down onto itself, even with the edge of the quilt top. (This is where the stitched angle makes a big difference in forming a perfect miter along the fold!) Begin stitching at the fold, backstitching to secure the stitches. Stitch to the next corner and repeat the process to miter the corner.

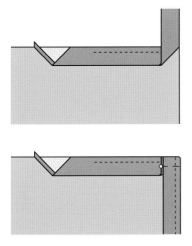

9. Stop stitching about 12" from where you began. Remove the quilt from the machine and place it on a flat surface. Fold one end of the binding back onto itself, and repeat with the other end of the binding. Butt the folded ends together and press the fold. Cut the strip on the right on the fold. Unfold the strip on the left and cut 2½" (or whatever binding width you prefer) away from the fold toward the end of the strip.

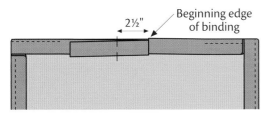

Fold back end of binding even with beginning edge.
Cut 2½" from the fold.

10. Open up both ends of the binding. Place the tails right sides together so that they join to form a right angle. Draw a diagonal line, and then pin the binding tails together.

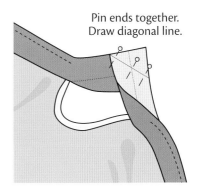

Pin ends together.
Draw diagonal line.

11. Stitch on the diagonal line. Check your stitching to make sure the binding lies perfectly flat on the quilt top. Trim the seam allowances to ¼"; press the seam allowances open. Refold the binding, aligning the raw edges of the binding with the edge of the quilt top, and finish sewing the binding in place.

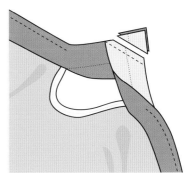

12. Fold the binding over the raw edges of the quilt to the back, with the folded edge covering the row of machine stitching. Hand blindstitch the binding to the quilt, mitering the corners.

*Imagination is more important than knowledge.*

Albert Einstein

This is the neutral quilt that began it all for me. When I showed it to the members of my Silver Thimble Quilt Club, it was a huge hit. The shop where I was teaching made kits, and they promptly started flying out the door! They kept cutting and cutting those kits. I think one of the reasons for the quilt's appeal is that the familiar Log Cabin enjoys an elegant spotlight when neutrals take the stage. And since the design and palette will never go out of style, it makes an ideal gift for a bride. I hope "White Chocolate" will be the beginning of your long and fruitful journey in making neutral quilts, just as it was for me.

### PILLOW PROJECT ONLINE!
You'll find illustrated, step-by-step instructions for making the coordinating pillow sham at www.martingale-pub.com/wrapped-in-comfort-pillow.

## Materials
*Yardage is based on 42"-wide fabric.*

¾ yard *each* of 6 assorted dark-value neutral fabrics for blocks

¾ yard *each* of 6 assorted light-value neutral fabrics for blocks

½ yard of medium-value neutral fabric for block centers

⅔ yard of fabric for binding

5¾ yards of fabric for backing

77" x 100" piece of batting

## Cutting
*As you cut, label and stack the pieces by number, so that each numbered piece will be easily accessible when laying out the blocks.*

**From *each* of the dark-value fabrics, cut:**

8 strips, 2" x 42"; crosscut *each strip* into:
    1 piece, 2" x 10½" (48 total; label as log 11)
    1 piece, 2" x 9" (48 total; label as log 8)
    1 piece, 2" x 7½" (48 total; label as log 7)
    1 piece, 2" x 6" (48 total; label as log 4)
    1 piece, 2" x 4½" (48 total; label as log 3)

**From the remaining dark-value fabrics, cut a *total* of:**

16 strips, 2" x 42"; crosscut into 48 pieces, 2" x 12" (label as log 12)

**From *each* of the light-value fabrics, cut:**

8 strips, 2" x 42"; crosscut *each strip* into:
    1 piece, 2" x 10½" (48 total; label as log 10)
    1 piece, 2" x 9" (48 total; label as log 9)
    1 piece, 2" x 7½" (48 total; label as log 6)
    1 piece, 2" x 6" (48 total; label as log 5)
    1 piece, 2" x 4½" (48 total; label as log 2)
    1 piece, 2" x 3" (48 total; label as log 1)

**From the medium-value fabric, cut:**

4 strips, 3" x 42"; crosscut into 48 squares, 3" x 3"

**From the binding fabric, cut:**

330" of 2½"-wide bias binding

**Finished Quilt:** 69½" x 92½" • **Finished Block:** 11½"

*Pieced by Teresa Wade; quilted by Beth Liotta*

## Making the Blocks

Each Log Cabin block consists of a 3" square surrounded by three rings (called rounds) of logs. After sewing each piece, press the seam allowances toward the just-sewn piece.

1. Lay out the pieces in numerical order, starting with a 3" medium-value square in the center as shown.

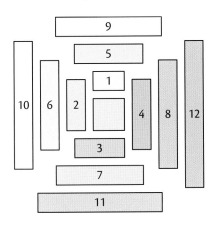

2. Sew piece 1 to the top edge of the center square, and then add piece 2 to the left edge of the unit. Add pieces 3 and 4 to complete the round, and then square up the unit as needed. The unit should measure 6" x 6".

3. Continue adding pieces in numerical order, squaring up the unit again after adding piece 8. The unit should measure 9" x 9". Sew the remaining pieces to the unit in numerical order to complete the block. When squared up, the block should measure 12" x 12". Make a total of 48 blocks.

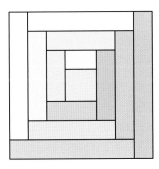

Make 48.

## Constructing the Quilt

Log Cabin blocks offer so many setting options; the quilt shown on page 20 is just one possibility. Try rotating the blocks to create a variety of settings, such as Barn Raising, Straight Furrows, or Streak of Lightning. Play with the design as you wish to achieve the setting that pleases you the most. I would love to see a picture of your finished quilt. My email inbox is always open!

1. Lay out the block in eight rows of six blocks each. When you are pleased with the arrangement, sew the blocks together into rows.

2. Sew the rows together and press the seam allowances in one direction.

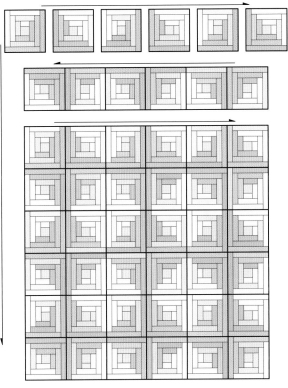

Quilt layout

## Finishing the Quilt

For detailed instructions on techniques for completing your quilt, refer to "Finishing School" on page 14. Use the 2½"-wide bias strips to make and attach the binding.

### NEUTRAL TABLE TOPPER

Here's a shocker! Believe it or not, I frequently utilize my neutral Log Cabin quilts as tablecloths. I've used them for everything from Christmas feasts to bridal luncheons. Am I worried about spills or mishaps? Nope. I worry more about damage when I use my grandmother's vintage linen tablecloths. I can make another quilt any time!

> *Whatever comes from the heart carries the heat and color of its birthplace.*
>
> Oliver Wendell Holmes, Sr.

In 2006 my husband and I built a new home in the suburbs of Atlanta. We live among warm stacked stones, weathered rooftops, and river rock in a neighborhood called HavenStone. This quilt makes me think of HavenStone and the wonderful nest it has become for us and our family. We celebrate our lives and future with joy and a home full of quilts! This quilt is destined to join us there.

## Materials

*Yardage is based on 42"-wide fabric.*

4¾ yards *total* of assorted dark-value neutral fabrics for blocks

3⅝ yards *total* of assorted light-value neutral fabrics for blocks

¾ yard of fabric for binding

5¼ yards of fabric for backing

76" x 93" piece of batting

## Cutting

*Use the A and B patterns on page 27, or use a 60° ruler and its side triangle companion ruler. I love the Tri-Recs rulers; they have markings that help make the units very precise. It's your choice, but whatever you do, have fun with it!*

**From the dark-value fabrics, cut:**

20 strips, 4½" x 42"; crosscut into:
   74 squares, 4½" x 4½"
   80 pieces using template A

20 squares, 6¾" x 6¾"; cut in half diagonally to yield 40 triangles

14 squares, 5¼" x 5¼"; cut into quarters diagonally to yield 56 triangles (2 are extra)

20 squares, 5" x 5"; cut in half diagonally to yield 40 triangles

20 squares, 4" x 4"; cut in half diagonally to yield 40 triangles

20 squares, 3" x 3"; cut in half diagonally to yield 40 triangles

40 squares, 2" x 2"

**From the light-value fabrics, cut:**

13 strips, 4½" x 42"; crosscut into 80 pieces and 80 reversed pieces using template B

20 squares, 6¾" x 6¾"; cut in half diagonally to yield 40 triangles

20 squares, 5" x 5"; cut in half diagonally to yield 40 triangles

20 squares, 4" x 4"; cut in half diagonally to yield 40 triangles

20 squares, 3" x 3"; cut in half diagonally to yield 40 triangles

40 squares, 2" x 2"

**From the binding fabric, cut:**

330" of 2½"-wide bias binding

### RESPECT THE BIAS!

Remember, when you cut squares in half diagonally, you're exposing the most vulnerable part of a fabric piece. Handle with care and don't wave the pieces around to all your friends. Bias, once stretched out, does not bounce back!

**Finished Quilt:** 68½" x 85½" • **Finished Block:** 12"

*Pieced by Becky Rabalais and Pat Wys; quilted by Leisa Wiggley*

## Making the Star Blocks

1. Use the dark A triangles and the light B and B reversed triangles to make 80 units as shown. Press the seam allowances toward the light triangles.

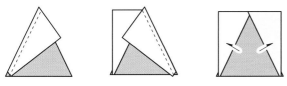

Make 80.

2. Lay out four units from step 1 and five 4½" dark squares as shown. Sew the pieces together into rows and press the seam allowances toward the squares. Then join the rows and press the seam allowances toward the center. Make 12 blocks. (Set the remaining triangle units and 4½" dark squares aside for now.)

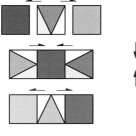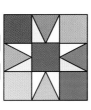

Make 12.

## Making the Snail's Trail Blocks

This block puts tons of movement in your quilt. Fabric placement is going to make all the difference–the light- and dark-value fabrics need to follow a trail. It's OK to mix up the fabrics, but make sure that the fabric values stay on the right path!

1. Use two 2" dark squares and two 2" light squares to make 20 four-patch units as shown.

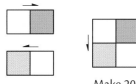

Make 20.

2. Fold two 3" dark triangles in half, and lightly crease to mark the center of the long side. Stitch the triangles to opposite sides of a four-patch unit, matching the crease line and seam line as shown. Press the seam allowances toward the dark triangles and trim the tips of the triangles even with the four-patch unit.

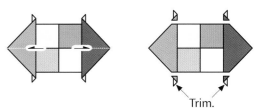

Trim.

3. Repeat step 2 using the 3" light triangles. Make 20 of these units and square them up to measure 4½" x 4½".

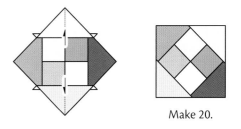

Make 20.

4. Repeat steps 2 and 3 using the 4" dark triangles and the 4" light triangles. Square up the units to measure 6½" x 6½". Then add the 5" dark triangles and the 5" light triangles and square up the units to 9" x 9".

5. Sew 6¾" dark triangles to the units from step 4, and then add the 6¾" light triangles to complete the blocks. Square up the blocks to measure 12½" x 12½". Make 20 blocks.

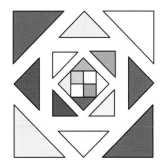

Make 20.

## Making the Setting Triangles

1. Sew one of the remaining 4½" dark squares to one side of a triangle unit as shown. Press the seam allowances toward the dark square. Sew a 5¼" dark triangle to the opposite side of the unit and press the seam allowances toward the dark triangle. Make 14.

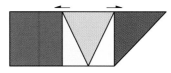

Make 14.

2. Sew a 5¼" dark triangle to a triangle unit as shown. Press the seam allowances toward the dark triangle. Make 14.

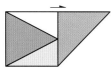

Make 14.

3. Lay out one unit from step 1, one unit from step 2, and one 5¼" dark triangle as shown. Join the pieces and press the seam allowances in one direction. Make 14 side setting triangles.

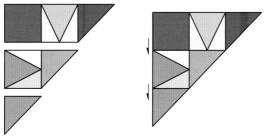

Make 14.

4. Sew 5¼" dark triangles to opposite sides of a triangle unit as shown. Press the seam allowances toward the dark triangles. Then add another 5¼" dark triangle to the unit to complete a corner triangle. Make four corner triangles.

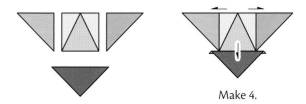

Make 4.

## Constructing the Quilt

1. Lay out the blocks, setting triangles, and corner triangles in diagonal rows as shown in the layout diagram.

2. Sew the pieces together into rows and press the seam allowances in opposite directions from row to row. Sew the rows together and press the seam allowances in one direction. Trim and square up the quilt top, making sure to leave ¼" beyond the outermost points of the setting triangles for seam allowance.

Quilt layout

## TAKE A GOOD LOOK

A diagonally set quilt can seem trickier to arrange and sew than a quilt with a straight setting. It's a good idea to lay out the blocks and study the arrangement carefully before you begin to sew. Move your blocks around until you achieve the perfect look. As you get up and down while sewing the blocks and rows together, think of it as sewing aerobics!

## Finishing the Quilt

For detailed instructions on techniques for completing your quilt, refer to "Finishing School" on page 14. Use the 2½"-wide bias strips to make and attach the binding.

*Back of "HavenStone." I scrap piece the back of my quilts all the time.*

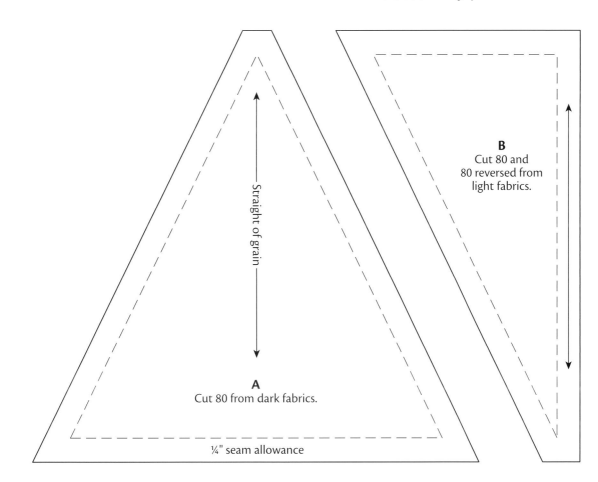

Straight of grain

**A**
Cut 80 from dark fabrics.

¼" seam allowance

**B**
Cut 80 and 80 reversed from light fabrics.

*There are two ways of spreading light: to be the candle or the mirror that reflects it.*

Edith Wharton

This quilt is the ideal candidate to show off a very special focus fabric you've wanted to use. "French Silk" was my first time using silk for piecing a quilt. I love the elegance of the fabric and the way it catches the light after it has been quilted. Don't be afraid of using silk— it's not scary at all. While you are making this quilt, whip up an indulgent French Silk pie, which happens to be one of my personal favorites!

## Materials

*Yardage is based on 42"-wide fabric.*

5⅛ yards of light floral print for blocks, inner border, and outer border

4⅝ yards of brown fabric for blocks, middle border, and binding*

¾ yard of tan print for blocks

5⅞ yards of fabric for backing

80" x 104" piece of batting

*\*If using silk, you'll need 4¼ yards of lightweight woven fusible interfacing.*

### DON'T GET RAVELED!

I used silk for the brown fabric in this quilt. If you choose to do the same, you won't be sorry with the results. I find that silk becomes much easier to work with if you stabilize it by pressing woven fusible interfacing to the wrong side of the fabric. A woven interfacing works best, but you can use a nonwoven if that's all you can find. Either way, it cuts down on the ravel factor, big time!

## Cutting

### From the light floral print, cut:

6 strips, 12½" x 42"; crosscut into 17 squares, 12½" x 12½"

9 strips, 3" x 42"

26 strips, 2½" x 42"; crosscut *18 of the strips* into 288 squares, 2½" x 2½"

### From the brown fabric, cut:*

20 strips, 4½" x 42"; crosscut into 158 squares, 4½" x 4½"

9 strips, 2½" x 42"

8 strips, 2" x 42"

350" of 2½"-wide bias binding

### From the tan print, cut:

9 strips, 2½" x 42"

*\*If using silk, follow the manufacturer's instructions and fuse interfacing to the wrong side of the silk prior to cutting strips.*

**Finished Quilt:** 72½" x 96½" • **Finished Block:** 12"

*Pieced by Pat Wys; quilted by Leisa Wiggley*

## Making the Snowball Blocks

Refer to "Folded Corners" on page 11. Draw a diagonal line from corner to corner on the wrong side of 68 of the 4½" brown squares. Place a marked square on one corner of a 12½" floral square, right sides together. Sew along the marked line and press the resulting brown triangle open. Flip the triangle back and trim away the corner fabric, leaving a ¼" seam allowance. In the same manner, sew marked brown squares to the remaining three corners to complete the Snowball block. Repeat to make a total of 17 Snowball blocks.

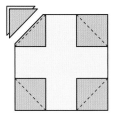

Make 17.

> ### WASTE NOT
>
> This is a great opportunity to make use of waste triangles. Sew a line of stitching ½" from the first stitching line as described in "Make Use of the Waste" on page 12. If you sew the waste triangles as you go, you'll have 68 additional half-square-triangle units to use in a bolster pillow (page 33) that you can make to coordinate with your quilt!

## Making the French Silk Blocks

To make the square-in-a-square units, you'll need 72 of the 4½" brown squares. Set the remaining brown squares aside for now.

1. Draw a diagonal line from corner to corner on the wrong side of each 2½" floral square, as described in "Folded Corners." Sew marked squares on diag-

onally opposite corners of a 4½" brown square. Press and trim. Sew marked squares to the remaining two corners to complete the unit. Make 72 units.

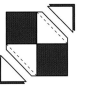

Make 72.

2. For the bar units, join a 2½"-wide brown strip and a 2½"-wide tan strip along the long edges to make a strip set. Press the seam allowances toward the brown strip. Make a total of nine strip sets. From the strip sets, cut 72 segments, 4½" wide.

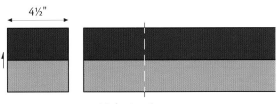

4½"

Make 9 strip sets.
Cut 72 segments.

3. Lay out one of the remaining 4½" brown squares, four square-in-a-square units from step 1, and four bar units from step 2 in three rows as shown. Sew the pieces together into rows and press the seam allowances toward the bar units. Join the rows and press the seam allowances toward the middle row. Make a total of 18 French Silk blocks.

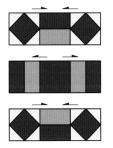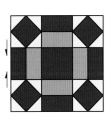

Make 18.

## Constructing the Quilt Top

1. Lay out the blocks in seven rows of five blocks each, alternating the Snowball blocks and French Silk blocks in each row and from row to row.

2. Join the blocks into rows and press the seam allowances toward the Snowball blocks. Sew the rows together and press the seam allowances in one direction.

3. Refer to "Adding Borders" on page 14. Join the eight remaining 2½"-wide floral strips end to end to make a long strip. Measure, cut, sew, and press the strips to add the inner border to the quilt top.

4. Repeat step 3 using the 2"-wide brown strips for the middle border and the 3"-wide floral strips for the outer border.

Quilt layout

## Finishing the Quilt

For detailed instructions on techniques for completing your quilt, refer to "Finishing School" on page 14. Use the 2½"-wide bias strips to make and attach the binding.

*Dreams and dedication are a powerful combination.*

William Longgood

**Finished Pillow:** 9" x 20"

## Materials

*Yardage is based on 42"-wide fabric.*

1⅓ yards of light floral fabric*

½ yard of brown silk or other dark-value fabric*

9" x 20" bolster pillow

18" x 30" piece of batting

60" of cording, ½" diameter, for piping

*\* You'll need an additional ¼ yard of both the light-value and dark-value fabrics if you aren't using leftover waste triangles.*

## Cutting

**From the light floral fabric, cut:**

1 strip, 18" x 30"

2 strips, 12" x 28½"

**From the brown silk or dark-value fabric, cut:**

1 strip, 2½" x 28½"

1 strip, 1" x 42"

60" of 2"-wide bias strips

### MAKING HALF-SQUARE-TRIANGLE UNITS

If you don't have waste half-square-triangle units, cut 14 dark 3½" squares and 14 light 3½" squares. Make and square up 28 units, following the directions on page 10.

## Sewing the Pillow

1. Layer the 18" x 30" floral strip with batting, baste, and machine quilt as desired. (I quilted a 1" diagonal grid.) You don't need a backing fabric because it won't show on the inside of the pillow, and backing would just add unnecessary bulk. A small project like this is a good place to play with those rarely used stitches! Or, how about hand quilting?

2. Cut the quilted strip into two 8½" x 28½" rectangles.

3. Using your waste half-square-triangle units, square up 28 units to measure 2½" x 2½".

4. Make two rows of 14 half-square-triangle units each, making sure to orient the dark and light triangles as shown.

5. Join the brown bias strips end to end to make a 60"-long strip, and press the seam allowances open. Fold the strip in half lengthwise, wrong sides together. Insert the cording, pushing it snug against the fold. Use a zipper foot on your sewing machine and set the needle so that it sews to the left of the foot. Sew the two cut edges of the fabric together, enclosing the cording. Then cut two strips, 28½" long.

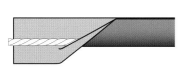

### JOINING COVERED CORDING

To reduce bulk and make a neater intersection when joining two ends of cording, remove about ½" of just the cording (not the fabric covering) from each end.

6. To make the ties, along one long edge of the 1"-wide brown strip, press ¼" to the wrong side of the strip. Fold the remaining long edge in the same way and press as shown. Then fold the strip in half lengthwise, aligning the folded edges, and

topstitch a scant ⅛" along the folded edges. Cut the strip in half, creating two 20"-long ties.

Topstitch.

7. Sew an 8½" quilted rectangle to each long edge of the 2½" brown strip and press the seam allowances toward the center. Join a row of half-square-triangle units to each end and press the seam allowances toward the center. Next add the covered cording to each end, aligning the raw edges of the covered cording and pillow top. Use a zipper foot to machine baste the covered cording in place. Finally, sew the 12"-wide floral strips to each end of the pillow front and press.

8. Fold over ¼" on each short end, and then fold over ¼" again to make a hem. Press and topstitch along the folded edge.

9. Fold the ties in half and place the folded end approximately 6" from each end of the pillow front as shown. Fold the pillow front in half lengthwise, right sides together, matching the seam lines and cording, and then sew along the raw edge using a ¼" seam allowance.

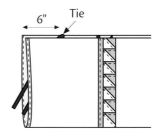

6"    Tie

10. Turn the pillow front right side out. Insert the bolster pillow form, twist and tie the ends like a Tootsie Roll, and adjust the gathers evenly.

*Be who you are and say what you feel because those who mind don't matter and those who matter don't mind.*

Dr. Seuss, pen name for
Theodor Seuss Geisel

I loved the idea of making a neutral, updated version of a classic French braid in a quilt—what a welcome change from standard block construction and classic block settings. This would make a wonderful gift for a graduate, signifying the exciting new road waiting to be traveled. And with its unusual graphic appeal, you might want to make one to warm up your own decor. It can be made larger without too much time and effort. When this quilt begins to come together, you'll discover that the possibilities are endless.

## Materials

*Yardage is based on 42"-wide fabric.*

4½ yards *total* of assorted light-value neutral fabrics for braids and setting triangles

2⅛ yards *total* of assorted dark-value neutral fabrics for braids and middle border

2¼ yards of light background fabric for sashing, inner border, and outer border

¾ yard of fabric for binding

5 yards of fabric for backing

71" x 86" piece of batting

## Cutting

If you want to start and end your braids with scrappy triangles, cut a 10½" square from a piece of paper, and then cut the paper square into quarters diagonally to make templates for quarter-square triangles. Use the templates to cut quarter-square triangles from your favorite fabrics.

**From the light-value fabrics, cut a *total* of:**

112 strips, 1¼" x 42"

2 squares, 10½" x 10½"; cut into quarters diagonally to yield 8 quarter-square triangles

**From the *lengthwise grain* of the light background fabric, cut:**

11 strips, 3½" x 81"

**From the dark-value fabrics, cut:**

7 strips, 1½" x 42"

56 strips, 1" x 42"

**From the binding fabric, cut:**

300" of 2½"-wide bias binding

## Making the Braids

1. Join two 1¼"-wide light strips and one 1"-wide dark strip along their long edges to make a strip set as shown. Press the seam allowances toward the light strips. Make a total of 56 strip sets. From the strip sets, cut 168 segments, 10½" wide.

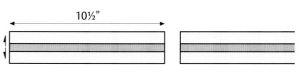

Make 56 strip sets.
Cut 168 segments.

**Finished Quilt:** 63½ " x 78½ "

*Pieced by Pat Wys; quilted by Leisa Wiggley*

2. To make each of the four braids, start by sewing a segment from step 1 to one short side of a quarter-square triangle as shown. Press the seam allowances toward the triangle.

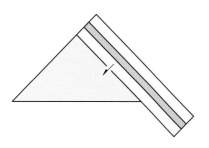

3. Add a segment to the adjacent short side of the triangle as shown. Press the seam allowances toward the triangle. Continue sewing segments to the unit, alternating from one side to the other, to create a braided chevron strip. Make four braids. Each braid should have a total of 42 segments.

Make 4.

**RELAX, DON'T WORRY!**

The edges of the braids won't look so great at this point. Have no fear; you'll trim up the long strips when they are complete, and they'll look perfectly beautiful.

4. Cut the remaining quarter-square triangles in half to make half-square triangles. Sew half-square triangles to the last two segments of each braid as shown. Press the seam allowances toward the triangles.

Cut.

5. Carefully press each braid. Trim the braids to measure 5¼" on each side of the vertical center. You'll find it easiest to trim the braid in sections, trimming one side at a time and continuing along the entire length of the braid. The trimmed braids should measure 10½" wide.

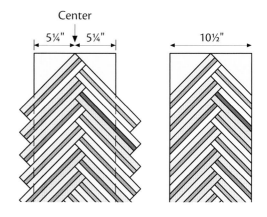

Center

5¼"  5¼"

10½"

## Constructing the Quilt

1. Measure the length of each braid; they should measure 64½" long. If they differ, calculate the average and consider this the length. Trim five of the 3½"-wide light strips to this length. Lay out the trimmed strips and the four braids, alternating them as shown in the layout diagram. Sew the braids and strips together and press the seam allowances toward the light strips.

2. Measure the width of the quilt top and trim two more of the 3½"-wide light strips to this measurement. Sew them to the top and bottom edges of the quilt.

3. Refer to "Adding Borders" on page 14. Join the 1½"-wide dark strips end to end to make a long strip. Measure, cut, sew, and press the strips to add the middle border to the quilt top.

4. Measure, cut, sew, and press the remaining 3½"-wide light strips to add the outer border.

### WHICH WAY? YOU DECIDE!

I chose to alternate the orientation of my braided chevron strips. This eliminated the directional look of the quilt and gave birth to the name "Going My Way?" Two travelers going in opposite directions meet, and who knows where they will end up! Of course, you may wish to create a more unified appearance by pointing all your braided chevrons in one direction. It's your choice.

## Finishing the Quilt

For detailed instructions on techniques for completing your quilt, refer to "Finishing School" on page 14. Use the 2½"-wide bias strips to make and attach the binding.

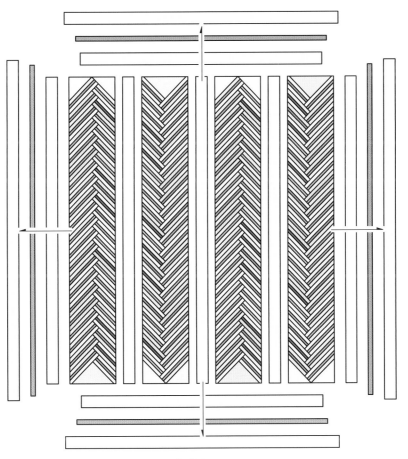

Quilt layout

*Ideas are like rabbits. You get a couple and learn how to handle them, and pretty soon you have a dozen.*

John Steinbeck

My love of scrappy projects is fully evident in this quilt. My friend Debbie made a quilt from this design as a wedding gift for her son and new daughter-in-law. They loved the neutral blacks and tans, which are a perfect addition to their new home. I was so honored that Debbie used my design for this special gift. The blending of a black-and-tan color palette with a scrappy fabric selection makes this quilt fun to create, and packs it with a big WOW factor. You'll hear oohs and aahs when you show this quilt to your friends. I promise!

## Materials

*Yardage is based on 42"-wide fabric.*

1⅜ yards *each* of 4 assorted light-value neutral fabrics for blocks and pieced border

⅝ yard *each* of 5 assorted dark-value neutral fabrics for blocks and pieced border

¾ yard of fabric for binding

5 yards of fabric for backing

74" x 86" piece of batting

### NO LIMITS HERE!

I've listed sufficient yardage to make this quilt using four different lights and five different darks. However, if you want an even scrappier quilt, use as many light- and dark-value fabrics as you can get your hands on. That's what Debbie did for her wedding gift. The sky is the limit. Get scrappy, you'll be happy!

## Cutting

**From *each* of the light-value fabrics, cut:**

3 strips, 6½" x 42" (12 total; 1 is extra); crosscut into:
    82 rectangles, 3½" x 6½"
    15 squares, 6½" x 6½"

3 strips, 4" x 42" (12 total; 3 are extra); crosscut into:
    60 rectangles, 2" x 4"
    60 squares, 4" x 4"; cut each square in half diagonally to yield 120 triangles

7 strips, 1½" x 42"; cut each strip in half to yield 14 strips, 1½" x 21" (56 total; 4 are extra)

**From *each* of the dark-value fabrics, cut:**

7 strips, 1½" x 42"; cut each strip in half to yield 14 strips, 1½" x 21" (70 total; 5 are extra)

12 squares, 4" x 4" (60 total)

3 squares, 2" x 2" (15 total)

**From the binding fabric, cut:**

300" of 2½"-wide bias binding

**Finished Quilt:** 66½" x 78½" • **Finished Block:** 12"

*Pieced by Teresa Wade; quilted by Leisa Wiggley*

## Making the Nine-Patch Units

Both of the blocks, as well as the pieced border, incorporate nine-patch units that measure 3½" square.

1. Randomly join two 1½"-wide, dark strips and one 1½"-wide light strip along their long edges to make strip set A as shown. Press the seam allowances open to reduce bulk. Repeat to make a total of 26 strip sets. From the strip sets, cut 336 segments, 1½" wide.

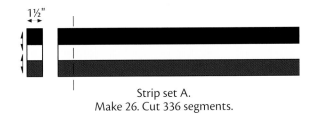

Strip set A.
Make 26. Cut 336 segments.

2. In the same manner, make strip set B using two light strips and one dark strip. Press the seam allowances open. Make a total of 13 strip sets. From these strip sets, cut 168 segments, 1½" wide.

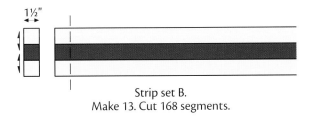

Strip set B.
Make 13. Cut 168 segments.

3. Sew a B segment between two A segments to make a nine-patch unit. Press the seam allowances open. Make a total of 168 units.

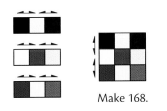

Make 168.

### PRESSING FOR PERFECTION

When making the nine-patch units, I find it especially helpful to press the seam allowances open. The seams within the units will match up more easily, and joining the completed blocks will be easier too. Trust me on this—I found out the hard way!

## Nines in the Corners Blocks

1. For each block, lay out four nine-patch units, four 3½" x 6½" light rectangles, and one 6½" light square.

2. When you're pleased with the value placements, sew the pieces together into rows. Press the seam allowances away from the rectangles. Sew the rows together and press the seam allowances away from the center. Make 15 blocks.

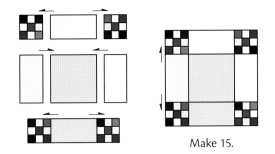

Make 15.

## Scrappy Nines Blocks

1. Lay out four 4" dark squares, four 2" x 4" light rectangles, and one 2" dark square as shown. Sew the pieces together into rows, and then sew the rows together. Press all the seam allowances open. Make 15 center units.

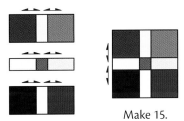

Make 15.

2. To make the pieced triangle units, sew 4" light triangles to adjacent sides of a nine-patch unit as shown. Press the seam allowances toward the triangles. The triangles are slightly oversized and will be trimmed in the next step. Make 60 of these units.

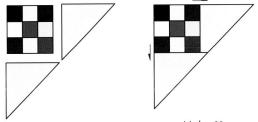

Make 60.

3. Trim the triangle units, leaving a ¼" seam allowance beyond the intersection of the nine-patch unit and triangles.

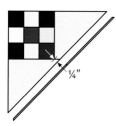

4. Sew triangle units to opposite sides of a center unit, aligning the point of the nine-patch unit with the center of the narrow rectangle. Press the seam allowances toward the center unit. Trim the tips of the triangles (which I call "bunny ears").

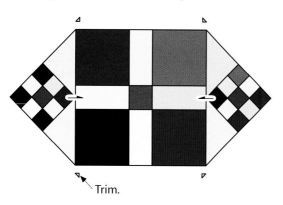

Trim.

5. Sew triangle units to the top and bottom of the unit from step 4 to complete the Scrappy Nines block. Press the seam allowances toward the center. Make 15. The blocks should measure 12½" square.

Make 15.

## Constructing the Quilt

1. Lay out the Nines in the Corners blocks and the Scrappy Nines blocks in six rows of five blocks each, alternating the blocks as shown in the layout diagram. Rows 1, 3, and 5 begin and end with Nines in the Corners blocks. Rows 2, 4, and 6 begin and end with Scrappy Nines blocks.

2. When you're satisfied with the arrangement, sew the blocks together into rows. Press the seam allowances toward the Nines in the Corners blocks. Then sew the rows together and press the seam allowances in one direction.

## Adding the Border

At first glance, it appears that this quilt doesn't have a border. But by adding borders of small Nine Patches and plain rectangles, you're adding an extra element that makes the design look finished. The border will use the 48 remaining nine-patch units.

1. Set four nine-patch units aside. Sew the remaining nine-patch units together in pairs. Make 22 pairs.

2. Lay out six 3½" x 6½" light rectangles, five nine-patch pairs, and two nine-patch units as shown to make a side border. Press the seam allowances toward the rectangles. Make two side borders. Sew these border strips to the left and right sides of the quilt top.

Make 2.

3. Join six nine-patch pairs and five 3½" x 6½" light rectangles, alternating them as shown to make the top border. Repeat to make the bottom border. Press the seam allowances toward the rectangles. Sew the border strips to the top and bottom edges of the quilt top. Press the seam allowances toward the borders.

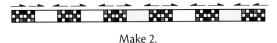

Make 2.

## Finishing the Quilt

For detailed instructions on techniques for completing your quilt, refer to "Finishing School" on page 14. Use the 2½"-wide bias strips to make and attach the binding.

Quilt layout

*Life is a great big canvas;*
*throw all the paint on it you can.*

Danny Kaye

The Summer Stitch In is an annual event I host in Georgia. We sew our brains out for six days straight, from 9:00 a.m. to 9:00 p.m. But sewing is only a part of it. It's really all about fellowship and friendship. Last year my friend Kristie came up with the inspired idea of sewing two Nine Patches together, and then slicing them into quadrants as you would a single disappearing Nine Patch. Wow! We each made our own quilt using this technique, and the rest is history. This quilt has the appearance of being complicated, but it's actually very fast and easy. I hope you enjoy making it as much as I did and will experiment using larger sizes of Nine Patch blocks. Thanks, Kristie!

## Materials

*Yardage is based on 42"-wide fabric.*

4½ yards *total* of assorted light-value neutral fabrics for blocks

4½ yards *total* of assorted dark-value neutral fabrics for blocks

¾ yard of fabric for binding

5 yards of fabric for backing

80" x 88" piece of batting

### SHUFFLE THE DECK

There are two reasons why I like to cut strips in half when sewing strip sets. First, sewing with 21"-long strips tends to be more accurate, lessening the chance of a wavy strip set. Second, this gives the opportunity to "shuffle the deck" with different fabric pairs, creating an even scrappier look for your quilt.

## Cutting

**From the light-value fabrics, cut a *total* of:**

41 strips, 3½" x 42"; cut each strip in half to yield 82 strips, 3½" x 21" (1 is extra)

**From the dark-value fabrics, cut a *total* of:**

41 strips, 3½" x 42"; cut each strip in half to yield 82 strips, 3½" x 21" (1 is extra)

**From the binding fabric, cut:**

325" of 2½"-wide bias binding

**Finished Quilt:** 72½" x 80½"  •  **Finished Block:** 8"

*Pieced by Pat Wys; quilted by Leisa Wiggley*

## Making the Blocks

1. Randomly join two dark strips and one light strip along their long edges to make strip set A as shown. Press the seam allowances toward the dark strips. Repeat to make a total of 27 strip sets. From the strip sets, cut 135 segments, 3½" wide.

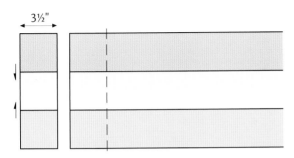

Strip set A.
Make 27. Cut 135 segments.

2. In the same manner, make strip set B using two light strips and one dark strip. Press the seam allowances toward the dark strip. Make a total of 27 strip sets. From these strip sets, cut 135 segments, 3½" wide.

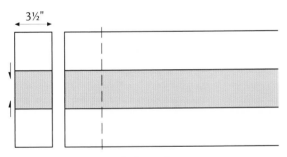

Strip set B.
Make 27. Cut 135 segments.

3. Sew A and B segments together as shown to make 45 nine-patch units with dark fabrics in the corners and 45 nine-patch units with light fabrics in the corners.

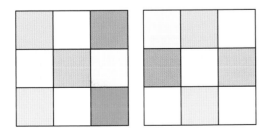

Make 45 of each.

4. Pair a dark nine-patch unit with a light nine-patch unit, right sides together, and sew along the left and right sides of the units as shown to make a nine-patch "tube." Make 45 of these tubes.

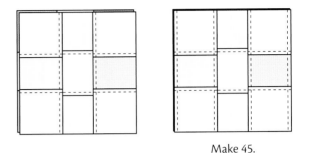

Make 45.

5. Cutting through both layers of the nine-patch tube, and measuring 4¾" from the raw edge, cut the units apart vertically and then horizontally without disturbing the units. Make 180 half-block units and press the seam allowances toward the large dark square.

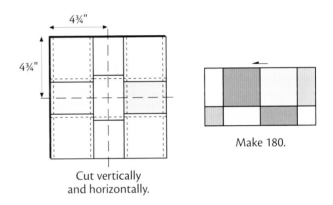

Cut vertically
and horizontally.

Make 180.

6. Set aside 36 of the half-block units to make border strips. Randomly join the remaining units in pairs to make 72 blocks. The blocks should measure 8½" square.

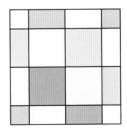

Make 72.

## Constructing the Quilt

I added a border of half blocks to complete my quilt. Of course, you might love the quilt without the additional pieced border, or you may choose to add a plain border.

1. Lay out the blocks in nine rows of eight blocks each. When you are satisfied with the arrangement, sew the blocks together into rows. Press the seam allowances in opposite directions from row to row.

2. Sew the rows together and press the seam allowances in one direction.

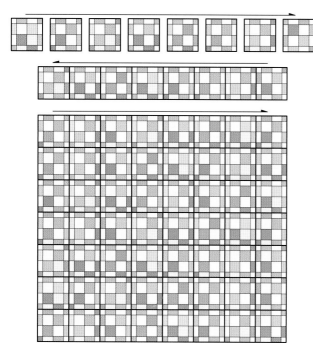

3. Join nine half-block units as shown to make a side border strip. Press the seam allowances in one direction. Make two.

Side border.
Make 2.

4. Join eight half-block units as shown to make the top border strip. Press the seam allowance in one direction. Repeat to make the bottom border strip. On the two remaining units, remove the center line of stitching to make four corner units. Sew corner units to the ends of the border strips as shown, paying close attention to the placement of the light and dark fabrics.

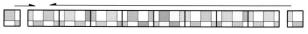

Top/bottom border.
Make 2.

5. Sew the side and then the top and bottom border strips to the quilt top. Press the seam allowances toward the borders.

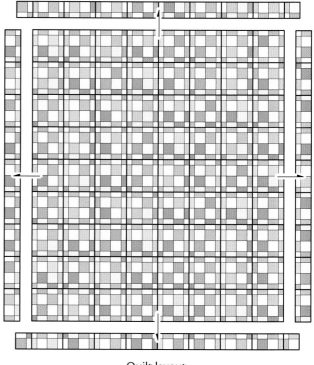

Quilt layout

## Finishing the Quilt

For detailed instructions on techniques for completing your quilt, refer to "Finishing School" on page 14. Use the 2½"-wide bias strips to make and attach the binding.

*We do not remember days,*
*we remember moments.*

Cesare Pavese

**Finished Pillow:** 30½" x 30½"

*Pieced and quilted by Pat Wys*

Thinking back, I remember making place mats with my own children and the children I taught in school. We wove paper strips through a base of construction paper that had slits in it. What fun we had, using these little woven works of art to decorate the holiday table for our mothers. I still have one that my daughter made in kindergarten! The construction of this pillow was inspired by those memories.

## Materials

*Yardage is based on 42"-wide fabric.*

3⅜ yards of assorted neutral fabrics for pillow center

⅝ yard of beige fabric for pillow-front border

1 yard of fabric for pillow back

25" x 25" square of batting for pillow front

28" x 34" piece of batting for pillow back

17" x 34" piece of batting for pillow back

4 pieces, 4" x 34", of batting for border

22" of hook-and-loop tape

24" x 24" square pillow form

Assorted buttons in different sizes and colors (optional)

Basting spray

## Cutting

**From the assorted neutral fabrics, cut:**

24 strips, 4½" x 25"

**From the beige fabric, cut:**

4 strips, 4" x 34"

**From the pillow-back fabric, cut:**

1 piece, 24" x 31"

1 piece, 13" x 31"

## Making the Pillow Front

1. Fold each 4½"-wide neutral strip in half length-wise, wrong sides together, and stitch along the long raw edge with a ¼" seam allowance. Press the seam allowances open, centering the seam in the middle of the strip. The seam allowances will not show when strips are woven.

2. On the 25" square of batting, measure down ½" from the top and lay 12 strips side by side across the batting square, with no space between the strips. Pin each strip in place to prevent it from moving. Machine baste along the left and right sides of the batting square, sewing ¼" from the edge of the batting, to secure the ends of the strips. Remove the pins.

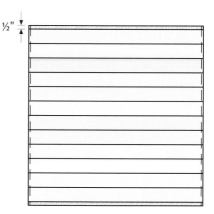

3. Weave the remaining 12 strips in and out of the horizontal strips, leaving no space between the strips. Alternate each row, placing the first vertical strip on top of the first horizontal strip, and then placing the next vertical strip underneath the first horizontal strip. The pillow center may feel a little floppy at this point but will be secured with the addition of the borders.

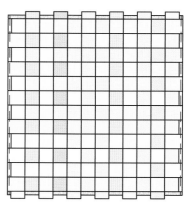

## Adding the Mitered Border

To secure the woven strips to the pillow front, you will stitch the ends of the strips into the seam line of the border. That way the strips will all stay in place and still have enough "give" to conform to the shape of the pillow form.

1. Following the manufacturer's instructions, use basting spray to adhere the 4"-wide batting strips to the 4"-wide beige strips. (The strips will be quilted after the borders are stitched to the pillow top.)

2. Fold the pillow top in half vertically and horizontally and pin-mark the center. Measure the distance from the center pin to each corner and write down the number.

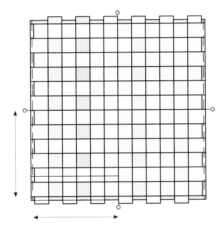

3. Fold one beige border strip in half crosswise, right sides together, and pin-mark the center. Using the measurement from step 2, measure from the center pin toward each end and pin-mark that measurement on each end of the strip. Repeat with the remaining border strips.

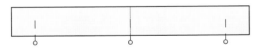

4. Matching the center pins on the border and the pillow top and the end pins to the corners of the pillow top, pin one border to the pillow top. Sew the border in place, starting and stopping ¼" from the edge of the pillow top with a backstitch.

5. Repeat step 4 to sew the remaining borders to the pillow top. Press the seam allowances toward the borders. The borders should extend beyond the pillow top at each end.

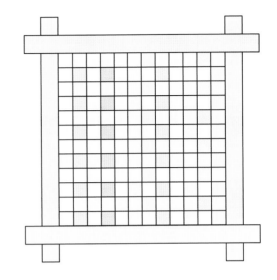

6. Lay one corner of the pillow front on your ironing board as shown. Fold under one strip at a 45° angle to the other strip. Press and pin.

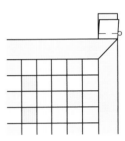

7. Fold the pillow front, right sides together, and line up the edges of the border strips. Stitch along the pressed crease, sewing from the inner corner to the outer edge. Trim the seam allowance to 1/4" and press the seam allowances open. Miter the remaining corners in the same manner.

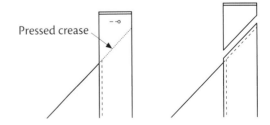

Pressed crease

8. Quilt the mitered borders as desired. I machine quilted straight lines, 1" apart, perpendicular to the border seam line. Square up the pillow top to measure 31" x 31".

## Assembling the Pillow

I quilted the pillow back before assembling the pillow to give it extra body.

1. Layer the pillow-back pieces with batting and baste. You don't need a backing fabric because it won't show on the inside of the pillow. Machine quilt as desired.

### FAST FINISHING

I'm all about getting small quilted projects like this one to the finish line in a jiffy. I love to use fabric basting spray for that very reason. On the pillow back, I machine quilted straight lines, ½" apart.

2. Fold over ¼" on one long edge of both backing pieces, and then fold over ¼" again to make a hem. Press and topstitch along the folded edge.

3. Fold the hook-and-loop tape in half crosswise to pin-mark the center. Fold each backing piece in half and pin-mark the center along the hemmed edge. Overlap the larger piece of backing about 1" on top of the smaller piece and match the centering pin of the backing pieces and the hook-and-eye tape. Sew the hook-and-loop tape to the hemmed edges of the backing pieces.

4. With the hook-and-loop tape closed and the two backing pieces overlapping each other, trim the pillow back to measure 31" square.

### TIME TO EMBELLISH

This is a good time to add some buttons or other decorative elements to your pillow sham. If you don't choose to add embellishments, I recommend that you hand sew a few tacking stitches at the intersections of the strips. You don't need to tack every intersection, only the first two or three rows around the outer edges of the pillow. Just be sure to stitch through the batting layer and hide your stitches as much as possible. The stitches help the strips lie flat along the curves of the pillow form. You'll be happy you took this extra step.

## Completing the Pillow

1. Place the pillow back on top of the pillow front, right sides together, and sew around the edges using a ½" seam allowance.

2. Clip the corners and turn the pillow sham right side out. Press and close the back using the hook-and-loop tape.

3. On the pillow front, topstitch along the seam line on all sides for a flange. Open the hook-and-loop tape and insert the pillow form through the opening.

4. You may want to add a few decorative buttons to the back of the flange as an extra finishing touch.

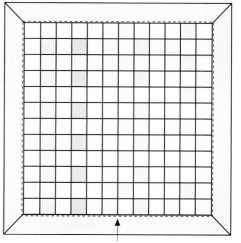

Topstitch.

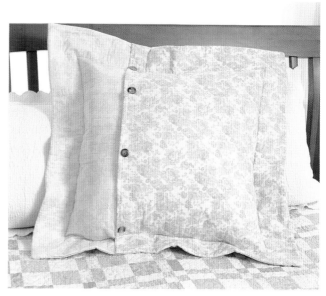

*Back of pillow*

*If you want a place in the sun, you've got to put up with a few blisters.*

Abigail Van Buren

This quilt is especially meaningful to me because my sister-in-law Patricia (Tricia) came to my rescue and helped with the construction of the blocks. I am so blessed to have a quilting buddy at every family celebration and as my close friend. We've known each other since we were 15 years old, and we married brothers, so we share the same married name!

## Materials

*Yardage is based on 42"-wide fabric.*

3⅞ yards of light background fabric for blocks, setting triangles, and binding

2¾ yards *total* of assorted medium- to dark-value neutral fabrics for blocks and setting triangles

3½ yards of fabric for backing

59" x 76" piece of batting

### SNEAKY, SNEAKY

I snuck a tiny bit of color into this quilt, using a mustard or gold shade in a few of the blocks. This subtle infusion of color makes your eye travel around the quilt without you even realizing it (an artist's trick I learned in college).

## Cutting

### From the background fabric, cut:

3 strips, 6½" x 42"; crosscut into 24 rectangles, 3½" x 6½"

5 strips, 4½" x 42"; crosscut into 36 squares, 4½" x 4½"

15 strips, 3½" x 42"; crosscut into:
    72 squares, 3½" x 3½"
    144 rectangles, 2" x 3½"

4 strips, 2" x 42"; crosscut into 72 squares, 2" x 2"

255" of 2½"-wide bias binding

### From the assorted neutral fabrics, cut a *total* of:*

4 strips, 2" x 42"; crosscut into 144 squares, 2" x 2"

18 squares, 6½" x 6½"

36 squares, 4½" x 4½"

10 squares, 3½" x 3½"

7 squares, 5½" x 5½"; cut into quarters diagonally to yield 28 quarter-square triangles

3 squares, 10" x 10"; cut into quarters diagonally to yield 12 quarter-square triangles

*For each block, you'll need one 6½" square, two 4½" squares, and eight 2" squares, all matching.*

### TRY THIS!

The cutting directions will yield the required number of triangles for the borders. I wanted to make the border very scrappy, so I cut a 5½" square and a 10" square from paper, and then sliced them into quarters diagonally to make quarter-square-triangle templates. I used the templates to cut triangles from the assorted neutral fabrics I used in the rest of the quilt. This gives the borders an even scrappier look.

**Finished Quilt:** 51" x 68" • **Finished Block:** 12"

*Pieced by Tricia Wys and Pat Wys; quilted by Leisa Wiggley*

## Making the Blocks

1. Refer to "Folded Corners" on page 11. Draw a diagonal line from corner to corner on the wrong side of the 2" background squares. Place a marked square on one corner of a 6½" neutral square, right sides together. Sew along the marked line and press the resulting background triangle open. Flip the triangle back and trim away the corner fabric, leaving a ¼" seam allowance. In the same manner, sew marked background squares to the remaining three corners to complete the snowball unit. Make 18 units.

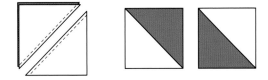

Make 18.

2. Refer to "Making Quarter-Square-Triangle Units" on page 10. Use two matching 4½" neutral squares and two 4½" background squares to make four quarter-square-triangle units. Trim the units to measure 3½" square. Repeat to make a total of 72 units.

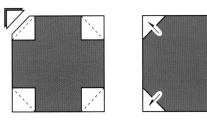

Make 72.

**SPLAY THAT SEAM, BABY!**

I love it when the center seam of any unit lies nice and flat. Refer to "Dispersing Seams Evenly" on page 11 to splay the seam allowances. Give it a try, and once you get the hang of it, you'll be splaying those seams from now on. Great to use in Four Patches too!

3. Refer to "Folded Corners" to draw a diagonal line from corner to corner on the wrong side of the 2" neutral squares. Place a marked square on one end of a 2" x 3½" background rectangle, right sides together. Sew along the marked line, press and trim. Make four matching units and four matching reversed units (36 total of each).

Make 36 of each.

4. Using matching units, sew one unit and one reversed unit from step 3 to a quarter-square-triangle unit from step 2 as shown. Press the seam allowances away from the center. Make 18 matching sets of four units (72 total).

Make 72.

5. Sew 3½" background squares to the left and right sides of a unit from step 4. Press the seam allowances toward the background squares. Make 18 matching sets of two units (36 total).

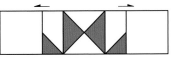

Make 36.

6. Sew two matching units from step 4 to the left and right sides of a matching snowball unit. Press the seam allowances toward the snowball unit. Make 18 units.

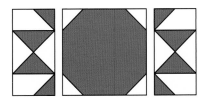

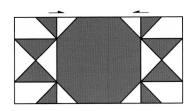

Make 18.

7. Using matching units, sew two units from step 5 and one unit from step 6 together as shown to complete the block. Press the seam allowances toward the center. Make 18 blocks.

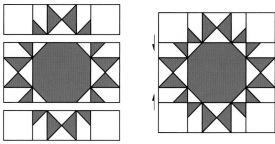

Make 18.

## Making the Setting Triangles

1. Sew a 3½" neutral square to one end of a 3½" x 6½" background rectangle. Sew a 5½" neutral triangle to the opposite end of the rectangle as shown. Press the seam allowances toward the rectangle. Make 10 of these units.

Make 10.

2. Sew a 3½" x 6½" background rectangle to the short side of a 10" neutral triangle. Add a 5½" neutral triangle and a unit from step 1 to make a setting triangle. Make 10 triangles.

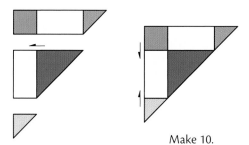

Make 10.

3. Cut the two remaining 10" quarter-square triangles in half to make four half-square triangles.

Cut.

4. Join a 5½" neutral triangle to each end of a 3½" x 6½" rectangle; then sew a half-square triangle from step 3 to the rectangle as shown to make a corner unit. Make four corner units.

Make 4.

## Constructing the Quilt

1. Lay out the blocks, setting triangles, and corner units in diagonal rows as shown in the layout diagram.

2. Sew the pieces together into rows and press the seam allowances in the opposite direction from row to row. Sew the rows together and press the seam allowances in one direction. Trim and square up the quilt top, making sure to leave ¼" beyond the outermost points of the setting triangles for seam allowance.

## Finishing the Quilt

For detailed instructions on techniques for completing your quilt, refer to "Finishing School" on page 14. Use the 2½"-wide bias strips to make and attach the binding.

Quilt layout

> *Go the extra mile. It's never crowded.*
> Executive Speechwriter Newsletter

Used as a wall hanging, table topper, or even a medallion quilt for a bed, this project will attract some attention. Use it all through the winter months to bring the season of beautiful snowfall inside your home. Buttons of all description make it extra special, along with rickrack inserted in the edges of the quilt. "Baby It's Cold Outside" will be a quilt you look forward to bringing out of the closet every winter!

## Materials

*Yardage is based on 42"-wide fabric.*

2½ yards of light gray fabric for block background

1⅝ yards *total* of assorted white fabrics for snow-flakes

3⅝ yards of fabric for backing and binding

1⅝ yards of lightweight fusible web

1⅝ yards of white lightweight fusible interfacing (optional)*

5½ yards of light gray ⅞"-wide cotton rickrack

56" x 56" piece of batting

Assorted white buttons in different sizes and colors for embellishment

Heavy cardboard or template plastic

* Refer to "Masking the Background" at right.

## Cutting

**From the light gray fabric, cut:**

9 squares, 16½" x 16½"

**From the assorted white fabrics, cut:**

8 squares, 11" x 11"
8 squares, 9" x 9"
11 squares, 6" x 6"

**From the lightweight fusible web, cut:**

8 squares, 11" x 11"
8 squares, 9" x 9"
11 squares, 6" x 6"

**From the backing and binding fabric, cut:**

210" of 1½"-wide bias binding

---

### MASKING THE BACKGROUND

Check to see if your background color shows through the white fabric; if it does, you'll want to "mask out" the background color. Cut squares of white fusible interfacing and iron them to the wrong side of each same-sized white fabric square. Then press same-sized squares of fusible web to the interfacing. You will be happy with the results.

---

## Making the Snowflake Blocks

1. Following the manufacturer's instructions, press the fusible-web squares to the wrong side of each same-sized white fabric square. Do not remove the paper.

2. Using the snowflake patterns on pages 68–70, trace each snowflake onto heavy cardboard or template plastic. Cut out the snowflake templates directly on the line.

3. Fold each fabric square in half, right sides together. Using the templates, trace the snow-flakes onto the paper side of each square from step 1. Make eight large snowflakes using the 11" squares, eight medium snowflakes using the 9" squares, and 11 small snowflakes using the 6" squares. Cutting on the traced line, cut through both thicknesses to make a complete snowflake.

**Finished Quilt:** 48½" x 48½"

*Pieced and appliquéd by Pat Wys; quilted by Leisa Wiggley*

4. Remove the paper backing and randomly arrange the snowflakes on each background square to create your own blizzard. Fuse the snowflakes in place, following the manufacturer's instructions. Make nine blocks.

Make 9.

5. Machine stitch along the raw edges of each snowflake using a thread color of your choice.

### KICK THOSE STITCHES UP A NOTCH!

I used a very small blanket stitch and monofilament. How about using some metallic thread with your stitches? You might even consider decorative stitches along the edges of the snowflakes. There are many ways to easily tailor this quilt to the decor of your home.

## Constructing the Quilt

1. Lay out the appliquéd blocks in three rows of three blocks each. When you are satisfied with the arrangement, sew the blocks together into rows. Press the seam allowances in opposite directions from row to row. Sew the rows together and press the seam allowances in one direction.

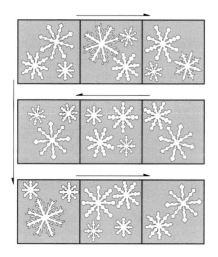

2. Layer the quilt top with batting and backing; baste. Hand or machine quilt as desired. Refer to "Finishing School" on page 14 as needed.

3. Add buttons, referring to the photo on page 62 for placement guidance. The buttons really bring the quilt to life!

### BUTTON BREAKTHROUGH

My friend Sandy stopped by my house when I was beginning to sew a bazillion buttons onto my quilt, and she showed me how to sew a button on with my machine! I knew it could be done but I'd never attempted it. To set your machine for sewing buttons, start by selecting a zigzag stitch and setting the stitch length to 0. To determine the stitch width, use the hand wheel (you don't want to break a needle) to carefully lower the needle into one hole of the button and then the other hole. Adjust the setting until you find the right width. Most buttons have a standard width between holes, which makes it easier since you won't need to keep resetting the width for different buttons. This method made sewing buttons so speedy, I was off to the races! Thanks, Sandy.

## Rickrack Binding

1. Center the rickrack lengthwise along the outer edge of the quilt front, and baste in place. At each corner, clip into the rickrack a bit so you can ease the rickrack around the corner smoothly. Fold and align the cut ends of the rickrack with the raw edge of the quilt top to make a smooth transition.

2. Sew the 1½"-wide binding strips end to end to make one long strip. Align one raw edge of the strip with the raw edge of the quilt top, right sides together. Sew along the raw edge of the quilt with a ¼" seam allowance, stitching through all the layers including the rickrack. At each corner, gently stretch the binding to ease it around the corner and make a gentle curve.

3. Fold the binding over the raw edges to the back of the quilt. Turn the raw edge under ¼" and hand stitch the binding to the back of the quilt, covering the row of machine stitches and one side of the rickrack.

# Winter Solstice Mantel Scarf

*Luck is a matter of preparation meeting opportunity.*

Oprah Winfrey

Winter takes on its own quiet splendor with this beautiful scarf. Adorning your mantel, it will sparkle the entire winter season while you keep warm inside. I used silk as the background fabric and crystals for decoration. Choose any embellishments to match this project to the holiday decor of your home. These frosty flakes will enjoy the spotlight all winter long!

## Materials

*Yardage is based on 42"-wide fabric.*

2½ yards of gray fabric for appliqué background and backing*

1½ yards *total* of white fabrics for snowflake appliqués*

1½ yards of lightweight fusible web*

1½ yards of lightweight fusible interfacing (optional)*

11" x 81" piece of batting

11" x 81" piece of freezer paper

Basting spray

Hot-fix crystals in several sizes and colors for embellishing (optional)

Drapery weights

*\*Adjust yardage amounts as needed to fit the dimensions of your mantel.*

## Cutting

**From the *lengthwise grain* of the gray fabric, cut:**

3 strips, 11" x 81"

## Making the Mantel Scarf

1. Using the pattern on page 67, align the curved edge of the pattern with the edge of the freezer paper and trace a continuous curved line along the length of freezer paper (or one that matches your required length). Cut on the line to make a template.

2. Lay the strip of batting on a table or other flat surface. Following the manufacturer's instructions, lightly spray the batting with basting spray. Place one of the gray strips, right side up, on top of the batting.

3. Iron the shiny side of the freezer-paper template to the wrong side of the second gray strip. Lay the strip on top of the first gray strip, right sides together, and pin in place.

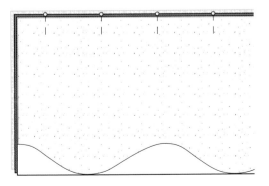

4. Cut along the curved edge of the freezer-paper template, cutting through all three layers. Remove the freezer-paper template and pin the three layers together again, aligning the raw edges.

5. Use a ¼" seam allowance to sew along the short ends and the curved edge as shown, stitching through all three layers. Leave the long, straight edge open.

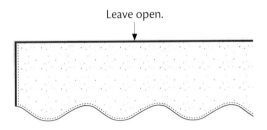

Leave open.

6. Turn the mantel scarf right side out and press.

## Appliqué

Check to see if your background color shows through the white fabric; if it does, refer to "Masking the Background" on page 61. For instructions on the following techniques, refer to "Preparing for Raw-Edge Appliqué" and "Stitching the Appliqué" on pages 13 and 14.

1. Using the snowflake patterns on pages 68–70, select the size and number of snowflakes for your mantel scarf. I used a total of two large snowflakes, eight medium snowflakes, and 10 small snowflakes. From the white fabric and the fusible web, cut squares as indicated for each snowflake.

   • Large snowflakes: 11" squares

   • Medium snowflakes: 9" squares

   • Small snowflakes: 6" squares

2. Following the manufacturer's instructions, press the fusible-web squares to the wrong side of each same-sized white fabric square. Do not remove the paper.

3. Trace the snowflake patterns of your choice onto heavy cardboard or template plastic. Cut out the snowflake templates directly on the line.

4. Fold each fabric square in half, right sides together. Using the templates, trace the snowflakes onto the paper side of each square from step 2. Cutting on the traced line, cut through both thicknesses to make a complete snowflake.

5. Remove the paper backing and randomly arrange the snowflakes on the mantel scarf. Refer to the photo below for placement guidance. Before fusing, trim the snowflakes along the straight edges even with the raw edge of the mantel scarf. Fuse the snowflakes in place, following the manufacturer's instructions.

6. Sewing through all the layers, stitch along the raw edges of each snowflake using a thread color of your choice.

## Finishing the Mantel Scarf

1. Using the remaining gray strip, fold over ¼" on each short end, press, and topstitch along the folded edge.

2. Layer the gray strip from step 1 on top of the appliquéd mantel scarf, right sides together and raw edges aligned. Sew the pieces together along the long edges, using a ¼"-wide seam allowance. Press the seam allowances away from the mantel scarf.

3. Turn the long, raw edge under ¼" and press. Fold the gray strip in half lengthwise, wrong sides together, and press. On the wrong side of the gray strip, sew drapery weights along the center fold.

4. Fold the gray strip in half again and slip-stitch the folded edge to the back of the mantel scarf, covering the row of machine stitches. Then topstitch the ends closed.

### EMBELLISH

This is the time to try some fun embellishments. I added hot-fix crystals, but you may wish to add buttons or decorative stitches. Rickrack, buttons, lace, and any other embellishments would be fun additions to the mantel scarf. The snowy skies provide limitless inspiration!

**Finished Size:** 11" x 80" (adjust to the size of your mantel)

*Made by Pat Wys*

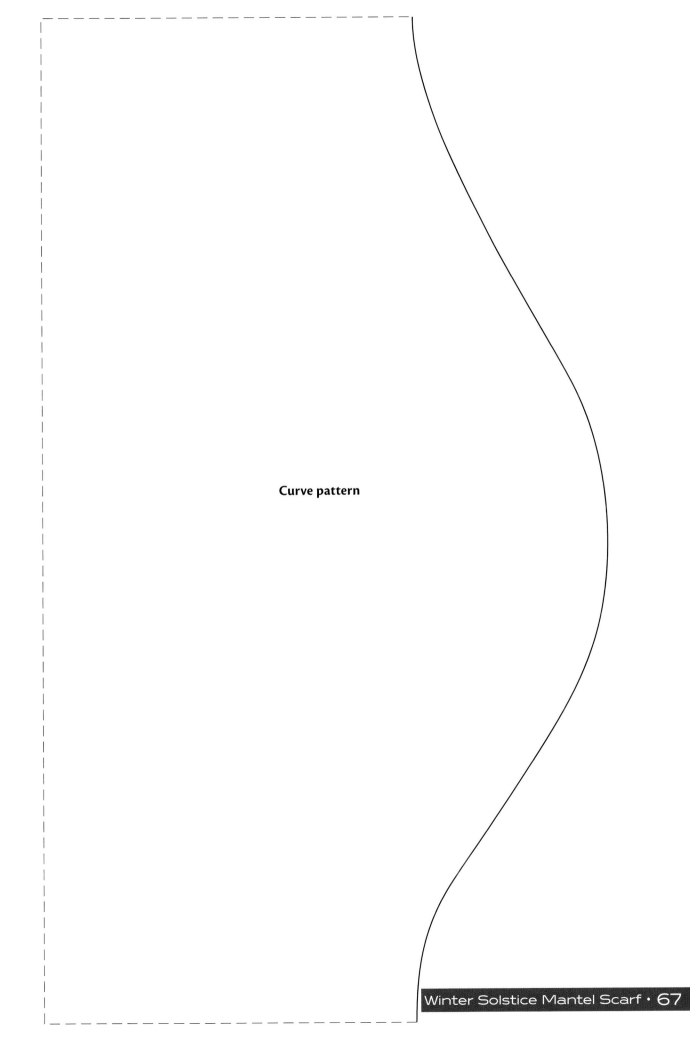

Curve pattern

Place on fold of fabric.

Flip pattern along this line to make complete pattern.

Place on fold of fabric.

Place on fold of fabric.

Place on fold of fabric.

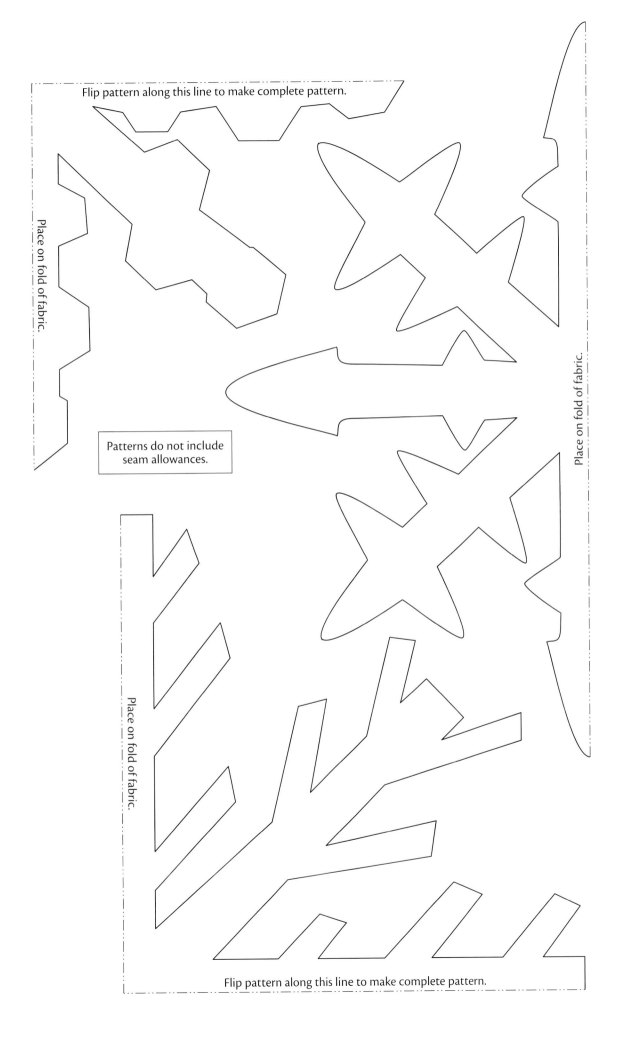

Flip pattern along this line to make complete pattern.

Place on fold of fabric.

Place on fold of fabric.

Patterns do not include
seam allowances.

Place on fold of fabric.

Flip pattern along this line to make complete pattern.

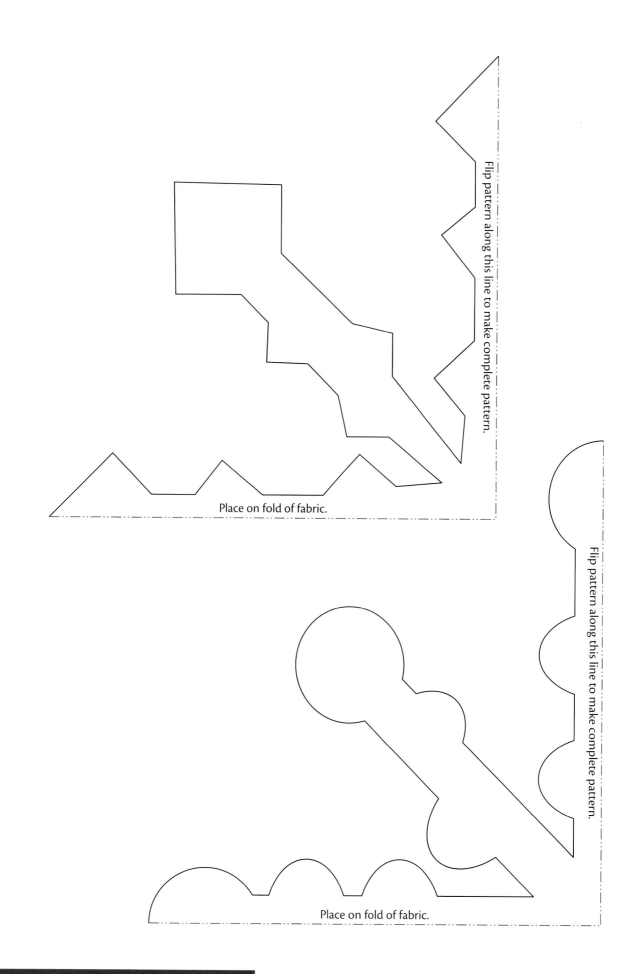

Flip pattern along this line to make complete pattern.

Place on fold of fabric.

Flip pattern along this line to make complete pattern.

Place on fold of fabric.

*The fastest way to reach new heights:*
*Just grab some string and fly those kites.*

Author Unknown

My grandmother Katherine, whose nickname was Kitty, was a very accomplished artist. I loved spending time with her drawing, painting, and learning so many lessons about art and life. I inherited much of her creative spirit and love of art. These whimsical baskets are reminiscent of an antique glass basket I inherited from her. On trips to antique shops over the years, I've added to my array of glass baskets. They are treasures to me, but the most important one in my collection is "Kitty's basket"!

## Materials

*Yardage is based on 42"-wide fabric.*

1⅞ yards *total* of assorted light-value neutral fabrics for block backgrounds

2¾ yards *total* of assorted medium- and dark-value neutral fabrics for appliqués and border

⅝ yard of fabric for binding

3½ yards of fabric for backing

61" x 61" piece of batting

## Cutting

### From the assorted light-value fabrics, cut:

3 squares, 13" x 13"; cut into quarters diagonally to yield 12 side setting triangles

25 squares, 8½" x 8½"

2 squares, 6¾" x 6¾"; cut in half diagonally to yield 4 corner triangles

### From the medium- and dark-value fabrics, cut:

4½"-wide strips in varying lengths, enough to total 210"

### From the binding fabric, cut:

230" of 2½"-wide bias binding

## Making the Background

Lay out the light squares, side triangles, and corner triangles in diagonal rows. Sew the pieces together into rows and press the seam allowances in opposite directions from row to row. Sew the rows together and press the seam allowances in one direction. The setting and corner triangles are slightly oversized and will be trimmed later.

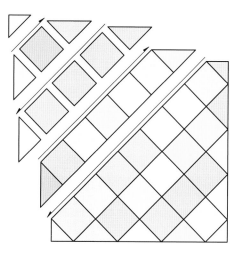

**Finished Quilt:** 53¾" x 53¾"  •  **Finished Background Blocks:** 8" x 8"

*Pieced, appliquéd, and hand quilted by Pat Wys*

## Appliqué

I made this quilt using the freezer-paper appliqué technique. However, if you prefer to use the raw-edge appliqué method, you'll need 3¼ yards of fusible web. Both techniques are described in "Appliqué" (page 12). Refer to the photo on page 13 for placement guidance as needed.

1. Using the medium- and dark-value fabrics and the patterns on pages 75–78, make four of each appliqué shape.

2. From the dark fabrics, cut 24 bias strips, ¾" x 16". To make the stems, place one end of a bias strip into a ⅜" bias-tape maker. Pull just the tip of the strip through the bias-tape maker and pin it to your ironing board. Continue to pull the bias-tape maker slowly along the strip, following closely behind it with your iron to crease the edges of the fabric as it emerges from the bias-tape maker. Make 24 stems.

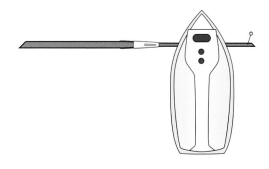

3. Repeat step 2, using 1" x 20" bias strips and a ½" bias-tape maker to make four basket handles.

4. Lay out one basket handle, one basket, and six stems in each corner, placing one or two stems underneath each handle; then appliqué the shapes in place. Appliqué the flower shapes in place working in numerical order.

5. After the appliqué is complete, carefully press the quilt center. Trim and square up the quilt center, making sure to leave ¼" beyond the outermost points of the light squares for seam allowance.

## Borders

1. Sew the 4½"-wide medium- and dark-value strips together end to end to make a strip at least 210" long.

2. Referring to "Adding Borders" on page 14, measure the quilt top through the center and cut one strip to this length. Sew the border strip to one side of the quilt. Measure the quilt top through the center, including the just-added border, and cut two strips to this length. Sew the strips to the quilt working in a counterclockwise direction. Measure the quilt through the center to determine the length of the last border, trim the remaining strip to that length, and sew the strip to the quilt top. Press the seam allowances toward the just-added border.

Quilt layout

## Finishing the Quilt

For detailed instructions on techniques for completing your quilt, refer to "Finishing School" on page 14. Use the 2½"-wide bias strips to make and attach the binding.

### BIG-STITCH QUILTING

I hand quilted "Kitty's Baskets" using two strands of taupe embroidery floss and stitches that are longer than I traditionally make for hand quilting. It makes quite a statement, and I love the way it looks. While I quilted, I was remembering my grandmother and celebrating her life with every stitch!

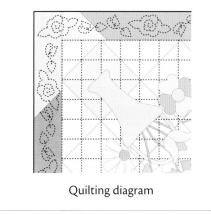

Quilting diagram

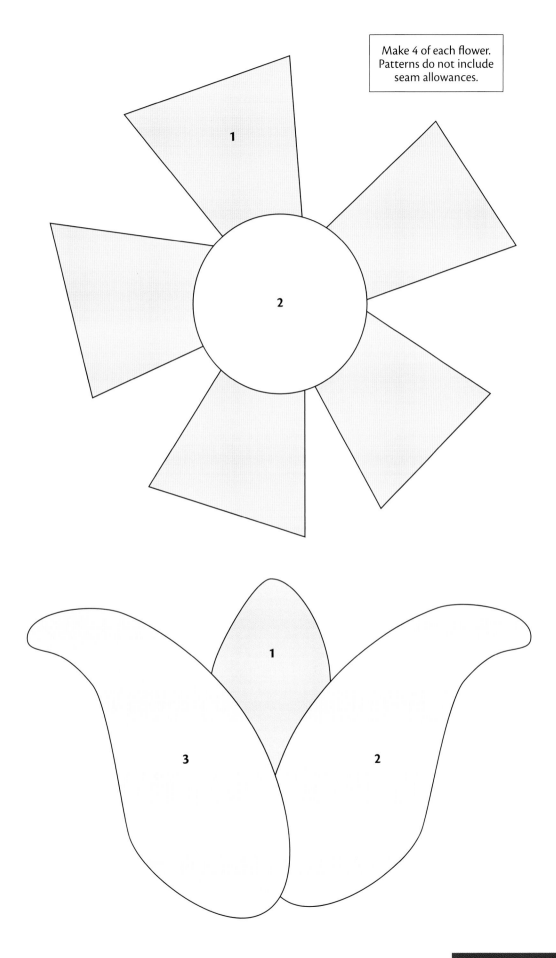

Make 4 of each flower.
Patterns do not include
seam allowances.

1

2

1

3

2

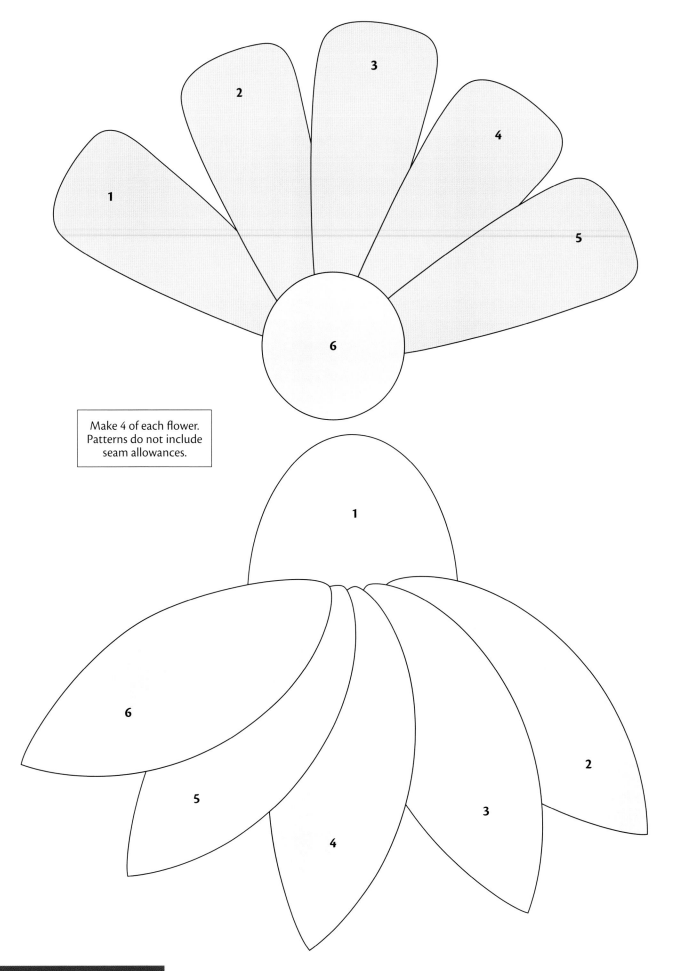

Make 4 of each flower.
Patterns do not include
seam allowances.

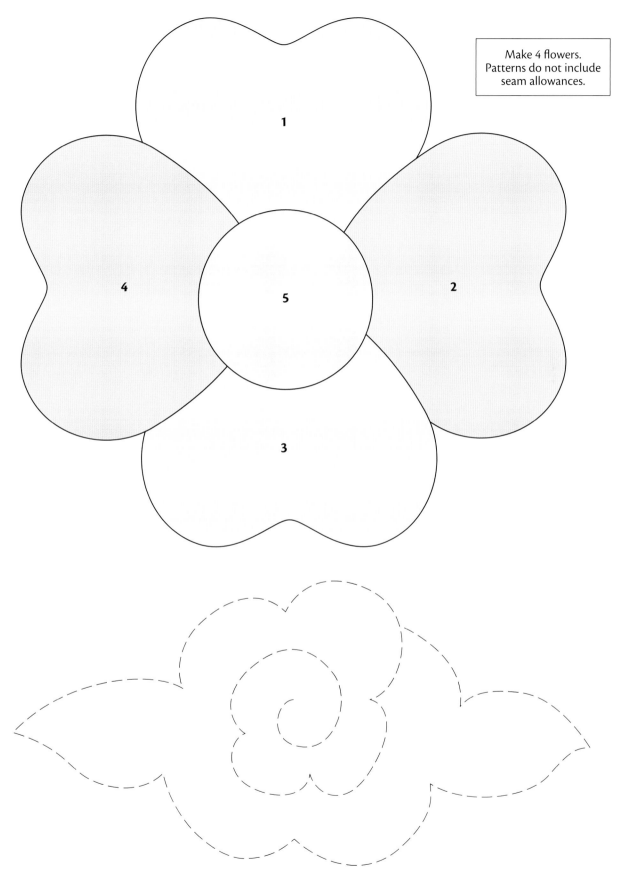

Make 4 flowers.
Patterns do not include
seam allowances.

1

4

5

2

3

**Quilting design for border**

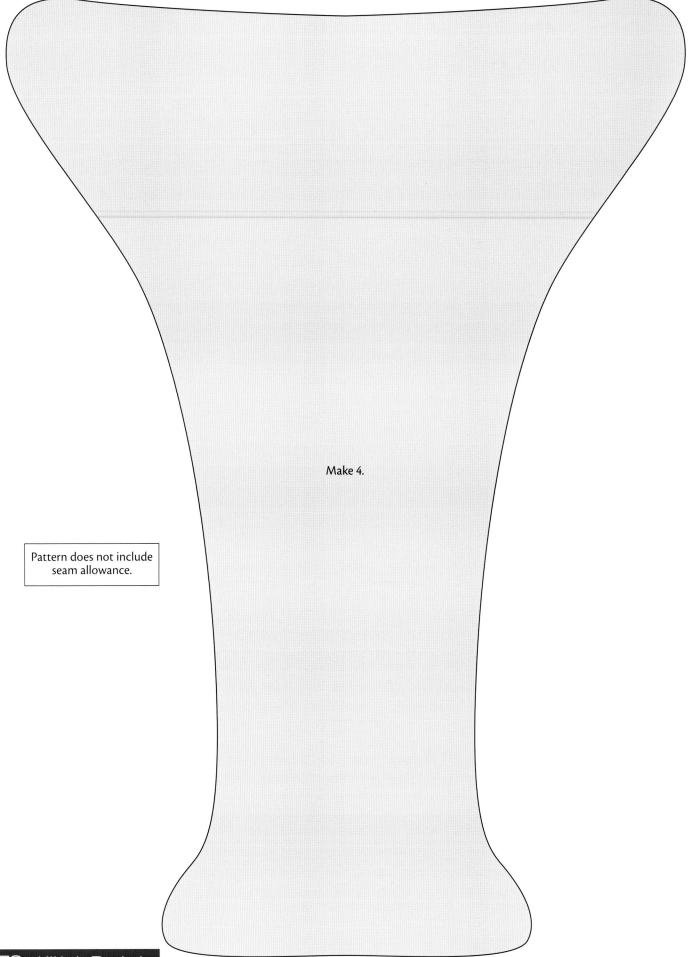

Make 4.

Pattern does not include seam allowance.

*The language of friendship
is not words but meanings.*

Henry David Thoreau

There are angels in my life, people who care, listen, and jump in to help when I need it the most. I can never repay these friends and family who have cheered me on and supported a dream, but I'm going to try!

Mary Ellen Von Holt—who helped a fledgling designer, advising, listening, and cheering me on. Your knowledge of the quilting industry is limitless and you share that knowledge in the most giving and helpful ways. You'll never know what a blessing it has been to have you as a mentor and what a treasured gift your friendship is to me.

Leisa Wiggley and Beth Liotta—your beautiful quilting amazes me, and the quilts in this book will be an enduring testimony to your artistry. Thank you for helping me finish those projects on time. I promise not to call you and begin the sentence with the word "rush" *(at least for a little while)*.

Suzanne Groover, Julie Miller, Debbie Frey, Cathy Adams, Anne Williamson, Teresa Wade, Melisa Morrison, and BJ Laird—thank you for the unconditional love and support you have given me. Thank you for listening and caring. We are a family and you are my beloved sisters.

My sewing angels Becky Rabalais, Kristie Michalowski, Teresa Wade, and Brenda DeBord—I would have surely ended up in big trouble and probably in tears if not for you and your sewing assistance! Without you, it might not have been perfect. Your thoughts and opinions are valued beyond belief. You are dear friends and you made me look good!

Tricia Wys—thank you for helping me with the sewing on "Here Comes the Sun." We married those two brothers, became sisters, and created memories. Quilting together makes our lifelong journey even more spectacular.

To Roger Boyer—thank you for taking the preliminary photos of my quilts. You take fabulous photos!

Each and every member of the Silver Thimble Quilt Club—you are the wind beneath my wings. You are the definition of what quilting, fellowship, and friendship are all about. Your support and encouragement will be kept and held deep in my heart forever. Each of your names are sewn with love into the stitches of every quilt in this book.

My dear longtime friends and book club buddies Jan Dillehay, Julie Miller, Sue Baum, Eileen Stevens, and Mary Carol Williams—you listened and let me have several passes on reading selections during the writing of this book. I love you more than you know. You have celebrated that one of the *Ladies of the Club* now has a number in the Library of Congress! I am determined to make quilters of all of you!

My new Martingale family, Mary Green, Cathy Reitan, Mary Beth Hughes, Karen Soltys, Nancy Mahoney, Tina Cook, and the entire staff of Martingale & Company—you are the best, and I am grateful for the opportunity to work with you on *Spotlight on Neutrals*. My dream has come true because of you!

Acknowledgments

79

*Photograph by Emily W. DeLoach, author's daughter*

Pat Wys holds a firm belief that people are truly blessed when they have a passion for work that calls to them, challenges them, and grows with them every day. Quilting is just that for her. She has seen and felt firsthand the healing, comforting, and uplifting power of quilting in the lives of many people. She's grateful to be a link in the joyous chain that connects us with quilters from our past and reaches out to quilters of the future.

Living in the suburbs of Atlanta with her wonderful husband of 38 years, Andy, they have raised two incredible daughters. Pat considers family the cornerstone of all things wonderful in her life. Quilting provides the whipped cream and cherry on top!

Pat graduated from Georgia State University with a degree in elementary education and a minor in studio art. Following graduation, she spent more than 20 years in both public and private education. She took her first quilting class in 1980, and quilting quickly became the center of her artistic interests. After years of learning the craft, she began teaching at local quilt shops and guilds. She found that her years of educational experience provided the foundation for a very natural progression into this new endeavor. The classroom is where she loves to be, and the title "teacher" will always be a source of pride.

As a frequent speaker, Pat leads many workshops and is a member of two active monthly quilting clubs in the Atlanta area. These are wonderful inspirations and modern-day quilting bees! In 2005 she started her own design company, Silver Thimble Quilt Company, which offers a number of new designs each year.

**THERE'S MORE ONLINE!**

You can find Pat Wys on her website and at her blog:
- www.silverthimblequilt.com
- www.silverthimbletalk.blogspot.com

Email us: info@silverthimblequilt.com

Find a *Spotlight on Neutrals* bonus project at www.martingale-pub.com/wrapped-in-comfort-pillow.